The Perfect Gangster

The Perfect Gangster

DJ Necterr

The Perfect Gangster

From the Streets to the Hip-Hop Industry

DJ Necterr

Poinsettia Publications

Poinsettia Publications
634 NE Main St
PO Box 1881
Simpsonville, SC 29680

ISBN 978-0615394473
LCCN 2010936683

Dedication

I would like to dedicate this story to those I've lost
and to those who may be lost in their struggle. It is
never too late to find your way.

"If you're going to judge me, then judge me, but
first become God and make everything better."

DJ Necterr

*Some names have been changed to protect the
innocent and/or the guilty.*

DJ Necterr

Prologue

The stress is swallowing him whole. Threats against him and his family assault him daily, and even those he once called friends are turning against him. He doesn't want to die, necessarily, but doesn't really care if he lives. His own family doesn't even like him, and he wonders how they'd feel if he was gone. He had started with six pills a day, then seven, then eight, mixing in an eight-ball of coke every day. On this day, he doesn't stop at eight. He takes pill after pill, pretending they are Skittles. He stops counting after fifteen.

He slips in and out of reality as memories swirl in and out of his vision like mini-tornadoes. *He's in third grade and at a wedding. Bullets begin to fly, and he watches in helpless horror as bodies start to fall. He tries to comfort his best friend and grasp what has just happened, never imagining his friend will soon be gone too.*

His body shakes violently, and he realizes he is lying on the floor staring ahead into the darkness under his bed. He tries to clear the fog that is invading his mind and ignore the strange sensation (is it pain?) in his chest. *He's ten years old and break dancing in the center of a group of young admirers who surround him on the playground. He*

DJ Necterr

remembers, feels, even, the exact moment that he knew hip-hop would be his life. Everything goes black just for a moment. His head feels like it's filled with lead, but he manages to move it slightly to the left. Eyes closed, he watches his middle school self as though he's watching a movie. *He's the DJ at a classmate's birthday party. He won't make any money, but he doesn't care. The bass pounds and the crowd dances and cheers as he contemplates what he'll play next.* Head spinning now, he feels like he may vomit and reaches for his phone, lying barely out of reach.

He begins to spiral down a deep dark hole and catches sight of himself again, now a teenager. *He walks the halls like a king. The school DJ, his pockets are now filling with cash cuz he gets paid for doing what he loves to do. He beams with pride thinking about his full schedule; parties, school dances, then spinning at the clubs every night all week. He should be tired, but he's not—he's living his dream and the adrenaline keeps him moving.* Something warm and bitter trickles out of the side of his mouth, bringing him back to reality for a moment.

What should he do? What can he do? Does he even care anymore? He stares straight ahead. Then darkness…and another scene starts rolling. *Dad is screaming about his grades, and he can hear Mom in the kitchen sobbing. He tunes them out and thinks only about his music. He knows that it is and always will be his life.*

He is unable to open his eyes now, but feels a smile forming on his lips as he watches himself, age seventeen, the winner of his first MC battle at Black Night, young and proud, his whole life ahead of him. The screen flickers before him, or is it just him trying desperately to open his eyes? *Cold hard metal around his wrists, he's pushed into the car that will lead him to his first experience with jail for drug trafficking. He watches his school neighborhood fade away out the back window and realizes he's not even eighteen years old yet.*

The film in his mind seems to be on fast forward now, and a flurry of scenes speed by. *Prison relationships and deals, the building of a major business, and his first love. His life has become one big party. Music, pills, after-parties, the most beautiful women in the world, and money...so much money! Everybody knows him now, and he is always surrounded by people—some friends, some wannabes, and some enemies in disguise. All of his hard work has paid off. He flies from city to city, hosting party after party for the likes of Jay-Z and Lil Wayne. Life is good.*

In the distance, or maybe right next to him, he hears a scream, and the voice is familiar. He forces open his eyes and spots his girl kneeling beside him, tears streaking down her face. She shakes him, but he can't speak. If he could, he

DJ Necterr

would tell her what he now knows. If he survives, he'll make sure life is different. He'll give up the street game and rely on his one true love. His music. Then sirens and a gurney...he loses consciousness and this time sees only darkness.

Necterr did survive. Just as he vowed to do when he faced death, he courageously fought to regain his health, and he turned his life around. He built his business and his life around what he loved most—the music. He now tours the country hosting shows with some of the biggest names in the business and promoting his own music. This is his story.

The Perfect Gangster

DJ Necterr

Contents

DJ Necterr

Chapter 1
How a True Boss Was Born

It was the early seventies, and there was a gangster in New York. Not really a gangster, but a businessman and a family man. They called this man King. They did not call him King because he was the king of his hood; nor was he the king of anything but his household with the birth-given name King. He was into small-time gangster crime like hand-to-hand drug sales. King was a local street dealer—mostly nickel-and-diming at the time, he'd occasionally get his hands on small amounts of cocaine and resell it as quickly as possible. He did what he could, taking his supply to the clubs, streets, and addicts' doorsteps.

He was no one big, and his life was pretty ordinary. Then one night at a club, he met a young lady by the name of Isis. She was a Latin and the sweetest girl he'd ever met. She was just beautiful. Standing about five-foot-seven, she had gorgeous flowing black hair and hazel eyes. She was slim with perfect breasts and a perfect butt, and had Brazilian lips. With the skin tone of Halle Berry and a stunning smile, she took King's breath away. An aspiring model, Isis had been trying for years to get into the modeling industry. Meanwhile, she had to make a living somehow, so she ventured into the night life and worked as a stripper. She worked mostly parties and was a hot young lady who had a thing for real black gangsters at the time. King and Isis fell in love at first sight, or at least that's how it felt at the time. They decided to be exclusive right away, though they both had many opportunities to be with other people. They spent every second they could together for eight months. Everyone knew them as a couple. In the middle of their ninth month together, they went to the courthouse and got married, surrounded only by a few of their closest friends and family. One short year later, in 1978, they had a baby boy and named him Jerome. They were in love with each other and their new son and couldn't have been happier.

When King had his son, Jerome, his life changed. He figured out that he needed to make a decision to work harder in his life. He wanted his son to have a better childhood and life than he had, and he was willing to do anything to make that happen. He knew of only one way to make a lot of money fast. He began to work harder than ever to come up in the ranks of street crime. He spent all of his time making more and better connections and proving to everyone on the streets that he was very good at what he did. He made it his personal mission to sell faster than everyone else. Once he had proven himself on his streets, he teamed up with other local dealers and began to partner with dealers in other cities. This meant he had to split his profits, but he could sell what he had much faster. Selling faster meant getting his new supply for a lower price. Soon his lower prices allowed him to sell his product cheaper and acquire more customers very quickly. Business was booming!

King had figured out how to move up very quickly in the world of street crime. He kept a very small group of associates and was very careful. He wasn't really a violent man at that time, but he realized that to truly prove himself to the drug bosses, he had to show them he was serious. He figured out that violence was a necessary part of being successful in the business. When someone double-crossed him, he had to go to the extreme to have that person harmed, so that everyone knew not to mess with him. When someone stole from him, it was up to him to make sure there was direct retaliation. He had to protect his reputation and recover his losses. He had to make sure he got revenge, and, most importantly, he had to make sure that everyone knew he was the one in charge. Unfortunately, this sometimes meant having these users killed to show that he was no punk in the streets. Of course, he always had an associate do the dirty work for him, but in the beginning, this violence bothered King a little. As he became more and more powerful and the cash started really rolling in, he got used to it. After all, he was just protecting his family and his livelihood.

In the early 1980s, King made the transition from doing hand-to-hand sales to becoming a major marijuana distributor. He had gone from selling nickel bags at an average of about 100 grams a week to selling about 100 pounds a week in less than two years. Just as his career as a dealer began to skyrocket, tension at home started building. Isis was busy raising Jerome and still working. King was bringing home more and more money every week, and while she knew he was dealing, she didn't realize the extent of his activities. She started to notice that they had to be very careful when they were out together. Her friends and family started to talk also. King was getting quite a reputation. She worried about his safety and the safety of herself and her son.

The business was what split their happy little family apart. King's stress grew as he had to start watching his back and worrying about his family nonstop. Other dealers were jealous of his rapid success, and there was always someone looking to rob him. Soon the threats started coming against him and his family. As the pressure grew, King became more angry and violent. He wanted the best for his family and was willing to do whatever it took to get it. Isis noticed he was changing and that they were starting to drift apart. She spent most of her time alone with Jerome, instructed by King not to go out because it wasn't safe.

King wasn't perfect. He was living the life of a dealer, and there were many other women. He was pretty sure Isis knew about them, and he felt a little guilty, but it was all part of doing business. Some of them were really into him, but he learned over time that most of them were gold diggers, using him for a good time and his money. He had his share of good times with them but was always very careful to protect his own family and business.

Isis was getting restless and becoming very unhappy. It seemed what little time they now had together they spent fighting. One night their fight was worse than usual. Isis cried and screamed about him being gone so much, about their lives being threatened, about the other women, and about him not even really knowing Jerome. She wasn't happy anymore and threatened to leave him. King had never laid a finger on her before, but he lost his temper and threw her against the wall, sending pictures shattering to the ground and waking up Jerome. He grabbed her by the throat, just like he'd done to many thugs on the street, and told her that if she ever left him, he'd kill her. Then he realized what he was doing to this woman he truly loved and stopped himself. He picked her up and hugged her, telling her how sorry he was. He told her that he had to finish up some important business, and then things were going to be different. He would go straight and find some other way to be successful. Isis tried to believe him as he gave her a kiss and headed out the door, and he tried to convince himself that it was possible to turn his life around.

When he left that night, little did he know that he was heading into a major trap. He sold to an undercover officer, and his business and life came to a screeching halt.

King was sentenced to three to seven years in jail. Isis was left behind to care for their son, deal with the fallout from his dealings, and try to make ends meet. She visited him all the time for a while, but then the visits started to slow down. She was sad and lonely, and just plain tired of the life she was living. In her mind, she gave up on King and set her sights on finding a new man. She had always had a man, and she was desperate to find a new one. She didn't know how to be alone. So it happened. She met a Latino man by the name of Richard Hernandez. Richard was a construction manager who made a decent living and had enough money left over each month to put into savings.

Isis' relationship with Richard didn't start like her relationship with King had. It wasn't love at first sight. There really wasn't much passion at all, but he was a good man. It was obvious to her that he cared for her very much. He also loved Jerome instantly. The two hit it off right away, and he began acting like a real father to her son within a couple of weeks. Richard treated her right and they did regular things together. "Regular" things were exactly what Isis was not used to.

DJ Necterr

With King, she always had to watch his back and her own. There were areas of the city they couldn't even go to for fear of being robbed or shot. There were clubs she couldn't go to with her friends because of King's reputation. Whenever she went anywhere with King, she had to walk in first and look around carefully to make sure there were no rival gangsters. She had been living her life for him and in fear. She was starting to wonder if she really had gotten anything in return.

So Isis started to get used to this new man and the regular things they did together. He took her to movies, to the mall, and out for dinner at nice restaurants. She didn't have to worry about being careful or threatened. She didn't have to watch his back or wonder if she'd make it home to her son at night. She fell in love with Richard and this new life.

In 1982, Isis gave birth to a second son and named him Eddie. Richard was a happy new father. He wasn't a gangster, and he took good care of the family. Isis was finally truly happy and secure. She had a man who loved her and two beautiful sons. She and her family were no longer in danger, and her love for King was quickly fading away. Her old life with King was becoming a distant memory.

Meanwhile, King was sitting in jail, wondering why his girl never came to see him anymore, and how his son was doing. He wrote her letter after letter but never got a response. He spent most of his time imagining her with other men, letting his rage take over his body and mind. He started to fill with anger and hate and thought of ways he'd kill any man who had been with his woman once he got out.

A year later in Chicago, another couple was deeply in love. Their names were Binky and Angel, and they had three beautiful children. Their youngest, JR, was born in 1981. JR immediately showed signs of being a great athlete someday. He was very athletic and loved anything having to do with sports. Erin was the oldest. She was born in 1972 and was Binky's daughter with another woman. Angel loved her as if she were her own daughter, though, and was a great mother to her. Necie was born in 1979 and was clearly the defiant child, but she always made them laugh. They were very happy and wanted to have one more child to complete their family.

On December 28, 1983, their wish came true—the couple had a son. The baby was a nice-looking dark-skinned baby boy. Angel and Binky instantly fell in love with this sweet, dark, beautiful baby, and they named him Nectorio.

Binky had dibbled and dabbled in the streets back in the sixties with his brother. They didn't do anything big; mostly they were just players. Angel wanted Binky to go straight when his fourth child was born, and he began to think about this a lot. He didn't want to lose Angel; he really loved her. He also knew that his current lifestyle would eventually just lead him to divorce and jail or prison. He was starting to see some of his friends and family die, and he knew he didn't want to be next. He had too much to live for. His oldest daughter, Erin, was becoming more and more aware of what was going on around her, and she was starting to ask questions. He wanted to be a good role model for her and for his other kids.

Binky decided that the only way to truly make a change would be to move his family to Los Angeles. There, he would be able to start over. He knew it had to be safer there than in Chicago. He also thought there would be many more opportunities for him and for his family. Most importantly, he felt that moving would save his marriage. He convinced Angel that it was the right thing to do, and they made the move in 1987.

Binky got a job at the train station, and some of Nectorio's earliest memories are of that place. He remembers visiting the station for the first time and looking in awe at the huge, fancy buildings. The trains roared past as he held tight to his dad's hand and they navigated through the massive crowds of people. He watched them all rushing around in suits and ties and dresses in a hurry to go somewhere, probably far away, he imagined. He sat quietly and proudly in the corner sketching pictures on a notepad and watching his dad work. During his breaks, his dad would buy him a soda and a treat from the vending machine and tell him stories about all of the crazy people that came through that place every day. After that day, Nectorio thought his dad had the coolest job in the world, and he decided that he wanted to do the same thing when he grew up. He wanted to be just like his dad.

Because Binky didn't know anything about LA and the city gangs that ruled some of the streets there, he wasn't too careful about where he chose to live. He unknowingly placed his family in a neighborhood that was in the middle of a gang war.

When Nectorio was five, he and his brother were playing in the family room when they heard several loud blasts. Nectorio had never heard anything like it, so he instinctively got down on the floor. His brother, a few feet away, did the same as their mother came running down the stairs to see what was going on. His mother's face instantly turned from anger to fear when she saw that the blasts had not come from them, but had come from outside. In an instant, something came flying through the window and Nectorio squeezed his eyes shut, trying to block out the sounds of his mother's screams and his brother crying. Then suddenly, silence. When he opened his eyes, he looked around for his family. He could see his brother's feet sticking out from behind a big black beanbag. Everything seemed to be in slow motion now, as he looked from the shattered window to the beanbag.

DJ Necterr

Their mother was crouched beside his brother rocking back and forth and sobbing. Nectorio spotted a hole in the side of the beanbag that hadn't been there a few minutes ago. A bitter lump began growing in his throat, and he thought he might be sick. Trying not to panic, he searched the floor around his mother for his brother's blood, holding his breath the whole time. Then his brother sat up. Nectorio could breathe again; his brother was okay. The beanbag had saved his life.

Nectorio's mother was not the same after that day. Her eyes didn't sparkle like they used to anymore, and she didn't smile as much either. She didn't allow the kids to go outside often, and she jumped anytime she heard an unfamiliar noise. She kept the blinds and curtains closed, and whenever a noise startled her, she would drop whatever she was holding or doing and yell for the kids to take cover. She was careful to stay low and away from the windows all the time. One day, Binky came home for an unusual extended lunch break and found his beautiful wife crouched on the kitchen floor with a loaf of bread, a jar of peanut butter, and a jar of jelly spread out in front of her on a towel. She looked up with fear when she heard the door open unexpectedly. She was making lunch for the kids the same way she did every day, but the sight broke his heart because he'd never seen her do it. He vowed to do whatever he had to do to get his family out of that neighborhood as soon as he possibly could.

In order to be able to afford to move to a better area of the city, Binky had to work more. He took a part-time job driving a bus. He regretted that he didn't get to see the kids very often, but he knew it would be worth it once they were living in a safer place. When he had rare time off from both the train station and his part-time driving job, he helped out his brother at his salon, giving haircuts. Though he had to be exhausted when he *was* home, he always made time for his kids. Sometimes, when the street was quiet, they'd go out and play catch or head down to the park for a family game of basketball. They'd meet Nectorio's uncle and cousins, and the ladies would sit in the shade and cheer for their boys. After some heavy competition, they'd have a picnic, enjoying the great food prepared by the girls and time spent together as a big, happy family.

Binky's focus was truly on his family now, and there were no other women or activities to distract him. The family was happy and at peace, and Nectorio, their fourth child, was well-adjusted and a happy young boy. None of them realized at that time that the happiness and peace would soon be shattered, and one more layer of Nectorio's childhood innocence would be stripped away.

Chapter 2
How Isis' Family Ended Up in Cali

Several years passed by, and Richard and Isis were building a great life together. Isis had two more children. She had another boy and named him after his father, Richard. They then had a daughter they named Ilene. Richard and Ilene made Isis feel even more like she had finally found a way to have a normal life. This family grew closer and closer, and they were very happy. There was only one problem. King had gotten out of prison.

King had plenty of time in jail to let his jealousy and rage grow. As soon as he got out, he began causing problems for Isis and Richard. He couldn't stand the fact that Richard had stolen his woman, and that they were a happy family while he was left with nothing. He knew he had to find a way to get his woman back and make Richard pay. He quickly reestablished himself on the streets and in his business, and then turned the rest of his attention to getting his revenge and getting Isis back.

First, King started breaking into their house. He did it mainly for effect; he wanted them to know he was out and not happy. The first few times he was subtle, moving a few things around and going through all of the closets and drawers. He wanted to learn more about the life Isis was leading without him. He also wanted them to know he'd been there, so he'd leave a picture overturned or smash a dirty glass he found in the kitchen sink. If he found something that he liked, such as Richard's gold watch or a piece of jewelry that looked even slightly valuable, he'd take it, not only to sell quickly for cash, but also to hurt them, if not emotionally, then financially.

It didn't take long for Isis to notice that someone had been in the house. She noticed the unlocked door first, then the shattered glass on the kitchen floor. She scoured the house then, trying to make sure nothing was missing and to convince herself that it was just a teenager or some inexperienced thief who hadn't found anything worth taking. She knew that this wasn't realistic and that a thief would've taken the TV, the DVD player, the stereo; yet she still tried to convince herself because the other option was King, and she didn't want to think about that.

Isis knew how angry he would be by now, at her and especially at Richard, and she tried to shut out the thoughts that he might try to take their son, Jerome, or hurt Richard to get back at her. No. It had to just be a random break-in. She'd have Richard change the locks and secure all of the windows, and they would move on. She wouldn't tell Richard that a single framed picture of her holding King's son was missing from Jerome's bedroom, and she vowed to replace it with a new one and never think about it again.

By snooping around the house and watching Isis and Richard coming and going with the kids, King quickly learned their schedules. He followed Richard to work, so he would know exactly where to find him when the time was right. On the way, he imagined himself in Richard's place with a normal job and his woman and child, and this only made him hate Richard even more.

Then the phone threats started. He'd leave messages on their answering machine, letting them know that he was watching them and had been in the house. He restrained himself a little during these calls, just in case his young son might be listening. He'd call Richard's cell phone and leave voicemails twenty to thirty times per day letting him know that his only goal in life was to mess him up. He threatened to destroy his home, his cars, everything he owned. When Richard would occasionally answer without checking the number first, King would threaten his life, letting him know that nothing would stop him from getting his son and his woman back. Richard threatened to call the police, and King told him he didn't care if he went back to jail, as long as he got what he wanted first. He let Richard know loudly and clearly that he better be watching his back at all times, and that he wasn't afraid to go after his family if necessary.

As the threats increased, Richard and Isis fought daily about whether or not to go to the police. Isis' old life was haunting her, and she was trying hard not to let it in. She now had to be careful again when she went out, especially with the kids, wondering if King was around and watching her. There was no doubt in her mind that he was dangerous; she knew what he'd done before he went to jail all for the sake of his business. She thought going to the police would only make things worse, and she begged Richard not to make the call. She desperately hoped that if they ignored his threats, King would get bored and move on to something else, letting them resume their normal lives.

Unfortunately, King only became more obsessed. He broke into the house once again, unsure of what he was looking for. He shattered a basement window and crawled through the tiny space, cursing Richard as he cut himself on the jagged glass. Now he was pissed. He dabbed at the blood on his arm and realized that this was all a waste of his time. He needed to take action. He made his way from room to room, overturning couches and chairs and smashing televisions. He pulled drawers out of dressers and dumped their contents into a heap on the floor. He left messages to Richard wherever he could, scrawling "You're Dead" across mirrors and furniture with a Sharpie.

He broke every dish he could find in the kitchen, smiling to himself when he pictured Richard coming home to this chaos instead of a nice home-cooked meal. When he felt as though he'd done enough damage on the main level, he headed upstairs, scrawling threats and profanities on the walls all the way up. The first room he encountered was the bedroom of Isis and Richard. He glared at the bed where they slept together; where Richard had sex with King's woman, then drifted off to sleep while King was with a different woman every night—mostly women who cared only about his money. The rage took over as he went to the closet and tore Richard's neatly hanging clothes down and ripped them to shreds. He went to the nightstand, ripped the alarm clock from the wall, and whipped it at the dresser mirror. The force wasn't enough to shatter it, so he found a shoe, a red heel, and broke the glass by hand. He tore the filthy sheets off the bed and wadded them up, adding them to the growing pile on the floor. On the newly bare mattress he wrote "Slut" and "Whore" in big black letters.

When he got to the kids' bedrooms, he wasn't even himself anymore. He threw toys and framed pictures and keepsakes against the wall and smiled as they shattered and slid to the floor. He realized he was holding a kitchen knife he'd carried up with him and used it to slash holes in stuffed bears and pillows. He'd finish one room and move on to the next, leaving nothing but destruction behind, not thinking of the innocent babies whose lives he was disrupting. The only room he didn't touch was the room of Jerome. When he was done, he didn't sneak out the basement window, risking another cut; he walked proudly right out the front door.

Isis got home first and immediately sent the kids into the backyard, hoping to shield them from the destruction. She was shaking when she dialed Richard's number and begged him to get home right away, unable to describe the damage before her and the fear she now felt for him, herself, and her kids. She knew that this time there would be no argument about whether or not to call the police, and she regretted ever fighting with Richard about it.

Richard was taking his usual route home when he noticed a black SUV following closely behind him. He wanted to get home to Isis and the kids as soon as possible, but he decided to take a turn off of his normal route to determine if he was really being followed. The Escalade turned when he did, and he was pretty sure King was in the driver's seat. He turned at the next set of lights and sped off into a foreign direction away from the city. He didn't want to face King now, while Isis was sitting at home scared and waiting for him. He also didn't know what King was truly capable of, though he'd heard stories from Isis and knew that the threats had been growing more frequent and severe every day.

King was right behind him and Richard had to think fast. He sped through the city streets, in and out of traffic, trying to lose King without getting into an accident. He thought he lost him a few times and prepared to turn back toward home, when the SUV would reappear in his rear view mirror. He had gone about fifteen miles when he decided he had to do something drastic. He peeled through a red light and sped off, watching King trapped at the light, unable to move into crossing traffic. He drove a few miles more to a secluded area and pulled over, looking around carefully to be certain he had truly lost King. He was shaking as he pulled out his cell phone and called Isis, letting her know she should keep the kids inside and lock all of the doors. He didn't call the police. He figured he had to get home to his family and calm down first.

Isis suppressed her tears and sent the children to Jerome's room, trying not to let them see the destruction on the way. She started to clean up the messes, telling herself she needed to be strong for her kids and her man. Maybe if it didn't look so bad when he got home, she'd be able to talk him out of going to the police. Now that she had calmed down, she was again convinced that it would be the wrong thing to do. She knew that King was furious, and that he had many connections in the city. Getting the police involved would only aggravate him more, and even if he went back to jail, he'd send someone else after them to get revenge.

DJ Necterr

When Richard finally arrived home, he couldn't believe what King had done to his house. Richard wasn't a violent man, but now he wanted revenge. Isis did her best to comfort him and somehow talked him out of going to the police. They did their best to get the house back to normal while keeping the details of what was happening from the kids. Surprisingly, things quieted down for a while. The threatening calls stopped, and King seemed to have disappeared. But that was just all part of his plan.

A month went by and Isis and Richard had gotten their lives put back together. King was not calling and Richard was starting to feel better about the situation. He could go to work again without worrying too much about his property and his family. He figured King had finally given up on getting Isis back.

One evening after work he met her at a restaurant, and they had a romantic dinner to celebrate; it was the anniversary of the day they had met, and they had survived many hurdles. After dinner, they were walking to the car when King appeared out of nowhere. Before she even knew what was happening, Isis was on the ground. King had shoved her out of the way so he could get to Richard. She screamed for help and was struggling to get up when she noticed something shiny in King's hand. He lurched at Richard as she tried to dive in between them. Now Richard was on the ground trying to fight King off, and she saw a stream of blood gushing out onto the sidewalk. She heard an onlooker yell to someone to call the police. King stood up and looked hatefully into her eyes, then ran off into the night. There was a crowd around them now, and she held tightly to Richard, praying for the police to get there soon, and for Richard to survive.

Richard was rushed to the hospital in critical condition. Isis sat beside his hospital bed telling the police detective everything she knew. She started with what she knew from when she was with King, and then told them about the calls, the break-ins, even the look in his eyes after the stabbing. She knew the risk of holding anything back at that point was greater than the risk of telling them everything. She wanted King put away, and she wanted her normal life back.

King was on the run again, and Isis and Richard were again trying to put their lives back together. The police had assured them that King now knew that they'd be looking for him, and he probably wouldn't come around. Richard knew better, and as he slowly recovered at home, he resolved to do whatever he needed to do to get his family out of danger. He knew that with all of his connections, King would find them if they just moved somewhere else in New York. He proposed to Isis, asking her not only to marry him, but also to

DJ Necterr

move to California, far away from King and his connections.

Isis had no problem marrying Richard, and she accepted his proposal excitedly. But the thought of moving across the country away from all of their friends and family terrified her. She convinced Richard to move to a different area of the city after they were married, and to wait it out and see if the police were right about King. She promised she'd still think about moving to California, but she wanted to try to make it work where they were, surrounded by friends and family.

Richard and Isis, now engaged, settled into a new home and neighborhood. It was a nice neighborhood on the other side of the city. Except for the fact that Richard had a longer commute to work, they really liked it. Life was getting back to normal and Isis began to let her guard down a little. She wasn't afraid to let the kids play outside anymore, and she could go out without worrying about running into King.

After a few short months of peace, the phone calls started again, but she didn't tell Richard. One day, when she was home alone, the phone rang and she answered to hear heavy breathing on the other end. She knew it was King, and this time, she made the threats. She told him that she would go back to the police and turn him in, and that she knew some of his connections and would turn them in too. Part of her knew none of this would matter to King, since he was already on the run, but she would do anything to stop him from disrupting their lives again. Her threats were empty. She didn't call the police. She knew they'd just tell her they were doing everything they could to find him. She didn't tell Richard that King had started calling again. He had enough to worry about. Isis tried to go on with life as she had before. She focused on being the best mother she could to her young children and hoped King wouldn't call again.

King, for the time being, shifted his focus back to his business. He knew he needed to let things quiet down with Isis and Richard before doing anything else. He couldn't afford to get caught and go back to jail. He regained his status as a dealer and partied hard with friends and women. Though he could have pretty much any beautiful woman he went after, he still felt angry and empty. There was one woman he didn't have, and he had to get her back.

Things had gotten pretty much back to normal for Isis, Richard, and the kids. Isis was at the store one day with her youngest son, who was toddling ahead of her in the toy aisle. Suddenly, a large man dressed in baggy black pants and a hooded sweatshirt picked up her son and walked toward her. She knew even before she saw his face, just by the way he walked, that it was King. Isis grabbed her son from his arms and looked up at him. His eyes were pleading this time, rather than filled with hate as they had been the last time she looked into them. He begged her to come back to him and told her that she'd be set for life. Business was good, and he loved her and wanted to take care of her and all of her children. She shook her head and backed away. King told her that if she didn't come back, he'd continue to make her life hell, and that he'd go after Richard again. Isis let him know that she wanted nothing to do with him, turned her back on him, and walked away. She hurried to her car, shakily buckled her young son in, and drove away.

Isis tried to shake off the encounter and focus on getting herself and her son home safely. She was about halfway home when she noticed a white car coming up behind her fast. She sped up and was trying to change lanes when she felt her car get pummeled forward. The white car was ramming her into traffic in the right lane, and her son was screaming in the backseat. She took another hit from behind, then one on the driver's side from a different car. Swerving away from King and the other moving traffic, she lost control of the car, went off the road, and crashed into a telephone pole. She felt her forehead and realized she had smashed into the windshield. She found her way out of the car and to the backseat where her son screamed. Several witnesses had pulled over to help, and King sat trapped in the smashed-up car behind her.

This is the day that King got arrested and went back to jail. It was also the day that Isis decided Richard was right. She talked to her fiancé, admitting that she couldn't take any more of this craziness. She was ready to move her family to California.

The Perfect Gangster

DJ Necterr

Chapter 3
How Two Families Collided

Sunshine state, palm trees, ocean breezes, Crips and Bloods; and a young Nectorio was ready to start kindergarten. As a child, Nectorio was bright, inquisitive, and loved music. He loved his family just as much and would do anything to make them laugh. He'd often set up his own makeshift drum set using pots and pans and anything else he could find around the house. He'd crank up the music and play DJ for his brother and sisters while they danced around the house. He was close to his older brother and already protective of his sisters even though they were older, and they clearly adored him.

Nectorio was excited and nervous on the first day of school. He hurriedly gulped down his breakfast as his mother packed him a lunch. On the way to school he gripped her hand nervously, and she smiled down at him and squeezed it gently, letting him know that everything would be fine.

The teacher stood at the door greeting all of the parents and her nervous new students. She was a pretty lady, with beautiful brown eyes and a dazzling smile. She made Nectorio feel more comfortable right away. With his outgoing personality, it didn't take long for him to meet some of the other kids, mostly girls, and he realized quickly that this school thing might end up being kind of fun.

At recess, things took a turn for the worse. Three boys were playing basketball, and it was clear that they had known each other before today, maybe even grown up together. One of them, Russel was really tall for his age and towered over the other two. Nectorio watched from a shady patch of grass by the fence as Russel bossed the other two around and hogged the ball. Nectorio wanted to play, but he didn't quite have the courage to walk up to them and ask if he could. Russel looked mean, and Nectorio didn't want any trouble on his first day. They were playing two on one, and Russel was clearly winning, though Nectorio would've called several fouls on him had he been the ref.

Suddenly, from out of nowhere, an awkward skinny boy about as tall as Nectorio walked out onto the makeshift court and asked if he could play. Russel shoved the boy out of the way so hard that he fell, and went in for a layup. Nectorio was on his feet, wanting to help the boy up; he felt bad and embarrassed for him. Russel's buddies, Julian and Rico—Nectorio had heard them say their names—yelled at the boy to get of their way, and he scrambled to his feet, adjusted his glasses, and said, "Come on, guys, couldn't you use one more player?"

Russel stopped playing then, and walked over to where the boy stood.

"You look like you'd be better off over there playing Barbies with the girls," he snarled.

Nectorio couldn't believe the kid could be so mean. After all, they were only in kindergarten. The other two were closing in on the boy now, and Nectorio's heart started racing. They wouldn't do anything to him, would they? He started to walk toward the little circle that formed around the boy. By the time he reached the outer edge, all three of the little bullies were taunting the kid who had just wanted to join their game. Nectorio couldn't believe what he was seeing when the scrawny kid reached out and shoved Russel hard, then kicked Julian in the shin. Stunned, all three boys just stared at him as he introduced himself.

"My name is Richard, and I'd like to shoot some hoops," he said as if he were introducing himself at a school play.

Nectorio couldn't believe it. He was shaking in anticipation of having to step in and maybe getting into a fight on his very first day of school, and this kid was totally cool and calm. Russel stood up and tossed Richard the basketball, and then looked over at Nectorio.

"What the hell are you lookin' at?" he said.

"He's my friend and he wants to play too," said Richard, to the amazement of Nectorio. "How 'bout it's me and him against you three buffoons?"

He smiled as he said it, and Nectorio thought he was about to get pummeled.

Russel smiled back at him. "Y'er on, and the winners get to use the ball and court the rest of this week."

Richard and Nectorio were an instant team and had an uncanny rhythm on the court for two people who had never even met before, let alone played basketball together. When they talked about it later, they discovered they'd both had plenty of practice building their skills with their brothers, one of many things they found out they had in common. They kicked butt on the court that day, winning the game ten to four. They mutually decided to share the court with the others the rest of the week, even though they had won sole rights to it. They knew it would be much more fun beating those three every day than just shooting baskets alone.

Richard Jr. and Nectorio grew to be best friends and became inseparable. They spent every day together during summers and hung out every night during the school years. They'd shoot hoops or practice pitching and catching in the alley behind Richard's apartment, or race up and down the city sidewalks on their bikes, building ramps out of scraps of metal and wood they'd found. Each set of parents treated each boy as if he were their own, feeding them both dinner, bandaging their cuts and nursing their bruises from their various adventures,

DJ Necterr

and laughing at the little schemes the boys came up with.

Richard's mom and dad, Richard Sr. and Isis, had settled back into a normal life. They had tried to make the move and transition as smooth as they could for their kids, who had already been through and seen so much. They had both gotten stable jobs and their kids seemed well adjusted once again. Everything was going well, and Isis just wanted one more thing to make her normal life complete. She had been engaged for years, but wanted to take the next step and get married. She finally talked Richard into setting a date. They set their wedding date for April 30, 1993, and Isis immediately began making plans. She was excited to plan for this next stage of her life.

While Isis had again started over and worked hard to create a normal life for herself and her family, King had plenty of time to think about her while he sat in jail. His anger and thirst for revenge was even stronger than it had been before, because Isis and Richard had sent him there. He relied on his connections to keep him informed about where Richard had gone with his family and what they were up to, and he patiently waited for the day that he would face Richard again.

Isis' and her family's excitement had grown as the wedding approached. She had planned a simple but charming event that involved her entire family. Her only concern was that the weather would hold out, as the ceremony was to take place outdoors.

Richard had other concerns. He had gotten word that King was scheduled to be released from prison in April, and he knew by now that King wouldn't be finished with him and his family. As the date got closer, he considered canceling the wedding, which he knew King would be aware of since friends and family from back home were invited. He tried to talk to Isis about it, but this only led to arguments. She didn't think King would have the energy or resources to come to California, let alone find them, and she believed he was probably finally over her. Richard remembered the hatred he'd seen in King's eyes, and he knew that King would stop at nothing to try to hurt him and his family. When their arguments turned to daily fights, Isis begged Richard to relax and drop it; he was ruining this most important time of her life.

Richard was right to be worried. King had found out every detail about the wedding down to how many people from New York had been invited. Unlike last time, as his release date approached, he wasn't excited about getting back to work building his business or worried about where he'd live. He was focused on a single date, April 30, and a trip he would make to California. There was no way Richard would marry his woman, and he wasn't about to let his son call that bastard dad.

Richard began obsessing more and more over King's release. He tried to hide his concerns from Isis, not wanting to upset her. He began researching other places to live in the city and even looked into getting a transfer to another state at work. He was sitting at dinner one night, pretending to listen to the happy chatter of his family, when he realized that he needed to be a man and not let King run him off the face of the earth. His family was happy here, and another move would devastate Isis and rip his kids away from their new lives and friends. He'd stay where he was and hope for the best, convincing himself that King had had plenty of time to get over Isis and his hatred for Richard, and that maybe he'd have better things to do when he got out this time around.

Isis remained oblivious to any possible threat or danger from King. She was wrapped up in planning her wedding, and believed nothing and nobody could stop her from having the perfect day she had dreamed of since she'd been a young girl. She believed that after all she had been through, she deserved to finally have her perfect day.

On April 20, King was released. He shacked up with friends, spent a few days getting caught up with several beautiful women, and then planned his trip. It didn't take him long to make a few quick sales, and he had enough to get to LA. He even bought a suit so he would look nice for the joyous occasion. He didn't tell anyone where he was headed, though most of his friends who knew him well had a pretty good idea. It was pretty clear that King didn't care about anything but revenge, even if it meant getting caught and put away forever.

The blessed day arrived, and everything was ready. Isis' dreams were finally coming true. As the music began, Richard stood in his tuxedo under a white flower-covered arch waiting for his bride. He looked around uneasily, sensing that something wasn't right, but then shook it off as nerves. All of the seats were filled with friends and family on both sides, and a white carpeted path covered with rose petals came up the middle—a nice touch by Isis.

As the music changed to an official-sounding wedding march, Richard spotted his little angel, Ilene, in a long white dress with glittery sequins sparkling in the spring sun. Her hair was piled on top of her head in ringlets, and she looked up at him and grinned as she led the way down the white path to the beat of wedding music and the ocean's waves crashing to shore.

Next, Richard's handsome young sons Jerome and Richard Jr. led their bridesmaids down the aisle. Richard winked at Jerome and a smile spread across his face. They had a great relationship; though Jerome knew Richard wasn't his biological dad, it hadn't mattered. He was the only dad Jerome knew, and he was good to him and his mother. Richard smiled proudly at his youngest son, Richard Junior, who looked so grown up and handsome as he took his place in the front. He caught Junior smiling out at his best friend, Nectorio, who sat in the front row on the bride's side with his family. Nectorio was such a part of Richard's family now that Richard wondered why he wasn't in the wedding too.

Nectorio was making goofy faces at his friend trying to make him laugh when a familiar sound erupted, interrupting the music, followed by screaming. The young boy remembered a day long ago in a small apartment, and a beanbag with a bullet hole in it, and realized quickly that bullets were flying everywhere as he saw people ducking and running and heard the screams of the crowd. He cowered behind the chair in front of him and tried to get a view of the front to see if his friend was still there.

Richard, the groom, ran down the aisle toward the shooter, who was standing only feet from where Nectorio hid. Nectorio felt as though he was watching a movie in slow motion as he saw what happened next. The shooter pointed the gun directly at Richard's chest and fired, and Nectorio watched his best friend's dad fall to the ground in a heap. Now in shock, the young boy waited for the shooter to turn around and shoot him or his parents, but he didn't. He just kept shooting at the man on the ground. He kept firing bullets into the man who had been like a second father to Nectorio and was the father of his best friend. Nectorio wanted to help, but he was frozen there and could only watch as the bullets hit Richard and his blood began to stain the white carpet. Beside him, he heard his dad whisper, "Stay down!" His mother was whispering a prayer, maybe the *Our Father,* to herself.

Suddenly, there was a flash of white, and Nectorio screamed in unison with someone else, maybe Richard Jr. or Jerome, as little Ilene ran to her dad, hoping to help or protect him. Nectorio closed his eyes and said a quick prayer, then stepped out into the aisle, hoping to push her out of the way. He was too late, though, and her little body fell to the ground next to her father's, as she was killed instantly by a stray bullet.

His mission accomplished, King fled the scene amid all of the chaos he had created. Wedding guests were running, screaming, and crying, and approaching sirens could be heard in the distance. Nectorio covered his ears and looked for his friend whose mother now sobbed over the bodies of Richard and her baby girl, Ilene, blotches of red beginning to stain her simple white gown. He spotted Richard Jr. hiding behind a large pot of flowers to the right of the scene, a look of shock and despair on his face. He ran to his friend and hugged him tightly, not knowing what else to do, and then Jerome grabbed them both and rushed them to a waiting car, hoping to shield them from the bloody scene. His efforts were in vain; neither of the boys would ever be the same.

The weeks and months that followed seemed to go by in slow motion. Nectorio stood behind his friend throughout his father's and sister's funeral. He tried to be strong for Richard, who was amazingly strong himself, never shedding a tear at the funerals. Nectorio knew that part of Richard had died along with his family members because his big flashy smile seldom appeared anymore, and he didn't talk much to Nectorio, or to anyone else for that matter.

Things got bad for Richard at home. His mother, Isis, never fully recovered from the tragedy. She lost her job and stopped being a mother to her remaining children. She rarely got dressed and spent almost every day sitting by the family room window looking out, as if she expected her lost husband and daughter to walk up the sidewalk and through the door at any minute. Nectorio watched Richard try to take care of her. If they were at Richard's for lunch, he would carefully make a tray of food for his mother and set it beside her. He tried not to make a big deal about it, but Nectorio felt so bad for him when the sandwich sat untouched hours later, and Richard would sadly remove the tray. Jerome had taken a full-time job and was rarely home because he was working, or maybe because it was just too hard to be there and see their mother like that.

It was several months after the funerals that Nectorio and Richard came home to another tragedy. They were excited because they had just beaten some guys from the neighborhood at a game of basketball. Richard was finally becoming his old self again, laughing and giving Nectorio a hard time. He challenged him to a game of Street Fighter. He ran upstairs to grab the Super Nintendo while Nectorio headed for the bathroom. Excited about the challenge they had planned and looking forward to kicking Richard's butt, Nectorio burst through the bathroom door and flipped on the light. Once again, he was in a bad movie as he looked at best friend's mother lying in a pool of dark red blood, empty pill bottles and a razor blade near her right hand.

Richard called down to him to hurry up and called him some dirty name, and Nectorio looked down at his shaking hands. He didn't know if she was dead or alive, and once again, he felt like he was frozen there, afraid to move, afraid even to breathe.

"Call nine-one-one," he uttered. Then he realized that he had barely made a sound and there was no way Richard could have heard him. So he tried again. "Call nine-one-one!" This time it was a scream, and had the situation been different, he would have been embarrassed at how frightened he sounded, almost like a girl.

Richard ran down the stairs, phone in hand, a look of sheer terror on his face. Nectorio pointed to the bathroom door, sad and angry that his friend had to see yet another family member lying in a pool of blood. This time there were tears as Richard began screaming his address into the phone. Nectorio wanted to cry too. He hated seeing his friend in pain again and, in a selfish way, wondered how long it would take him to bounce back this time.

Jerome was called next, and the three boys watched in silence as Isis was carried away in the ambulance. The EMTs had assured the brothers that their mother would probably be okay. Richard and Nectorio cleaned up the mess in the bathroom while Jerome called friends and relatives. Then Jerome had to head back to work. Nectorio convinced Richard to come home with him and stay there for a few days, assuring him that his parents would be happy to have him.

A few days ended up being several weeks. Nectorio's parents took Richard in and treated him like part of the family. He was very polite and grateful but would get into unusually quiet moods sometimes. Nectorio knew he was thinking about his family and tried to leave him alone during those times. Almost every night, Richard would wake the family up with his piercing screams, and Nectorio's mother, Angel, would race to his makeshift bed on the couch to comfort him back to sleep. He was haunted by nightmares, and Nectorio knew they were probably bloody images of his dad, his little sister, and his mother.

Nectorio tried to distract Richard by keeping him busy. They played ball with the other guys in the neighborhood, and he spent lots of time trying to teach Richard his new break-dancing moves. Crowds of kids would form around them out on the street the minute they turned the music on. Sometimes he would catch Richard smiling when the girls would form a circle around them clapping, singing, and cheering them on, but those smiles were rare these days. Richard was changing.

When Isis got home, things returned to normal for a few weeks. Richard seemed to be happier, and Nectorio felt like maybe his friend would be okay. After three weeks, Isis tried to commit suicide again. Then two weeks home, and another attempt on her life. After the fifth suicide attempt, she never came home. She ended up in a mental institute, which left the children to fend for themselves. Since Richard was so young, social services had to get involved to help sort things out. Richard was sent into foster care, and Nectorio had now lost his very best and only friend.

Chapter 4
Growing Up

Nectorio grew up in a well-conditioned home. His family lived in Moreno Valley, California. Angel worked as a human resources manager at a construction company in Perris, California, and Binky was a bus driver in San Bernardino. Both of them pretty much worked from nine to five so they could be home for the kids in the evenings and as involved as possible in their lives. They attended sporting events, proudly cheering their kids on, and never missed a parent-teacher conference.

Nectorio was into a lot of sports. He had a sport for every season, playing basketball, baseball, soccer, and football. Like his brother, he was a natural and did very well without having to exert too much effort. He excelled on each team, and his parents supported him and were very proud of him, especially when he made the All Stars, which he did for every sport. He made some friends on each team, but none of them really became close friends; he figured this was because they were jealous of his talent.

Witnessing the tragedy he had, though, made him change. Though he tried not to think about it, thoughts of everything that had happened to Richard and his family always crept into his mind. These horrible images and memories robbed him of the happiness he had once felt from doing well in school and at sports. He soon started going down a whole different route, driven by emotions he didn't know how to control. He couldn't understand why good people like Richard and Ilene had to die, and why his best friend had been taken away from him. Anger, bitterness, and confusion started to grow inside of him, and although he hid it from his family for a while, he started to act differently. He searched for new friends even though he knew nobody could ever replace Richard.

By the time he reached fifth grade, Nectorio had started smoking and drinking. Richard was gone, and playing basketball only reminded him of his lost friend and made him wonder where he was. This sadness always turned to anger, and Nectorio had a hard time finding ways to control that anger. He had to find ways to forget what had happened. He had no other real friends, so he gravitated toward the partiers. They were other bitter and angry kids all trying to forget or run from something they had experienced. They weren't the types of kids who played sports or tried out for school plays.

Nectorio started by smoking. He loved the thrill of doing something he wasn't supposed to be doing and of working to not get caught. He'd meet his new friends under the freeway bridge or at the park after school, and he quickly learned to smoke. Much like sports, this new skill came easily to him, and while some of the other guys choked and gagged every time they took a hit, Nectorio was smooth, and looked like he'd been doing it all his life. It didn't take long for him to earn their admiration. He started to carry a bottle of cologne with him to hide the smell, and most days, the boys would go swimming afterwards, a fun alternative to a shower that got rid of any lingering odors.

When the thrill of smoking wore off, the boys started to experiment with alcohol. Nectorio's new friends would invite him over when their parents were gone and they'd raid the liquor cabinets, drinking whatever they could get their hands on, then replacing the missing alcohol with water or soda. He learned to carry extra packs of gum with him, and even mouthwash sometimes. He knew that the smell of alcohol couldn't be erased as easily as smoke by a swim in the lake. Nectorio liked the way the alcohol made him feel. It numbed his pain and made all of the bad feelings and memories disappear for a while. When he was drinking with his new friends, they would almost measure up to Richard. Then he felt like he was lucky because he had gained several new friends instead of just being the kid who had lost one best friend. That lucky feeling always wore off with the buzz, though, leaving him feeling even more alone than before.

In sixth grade, Nectorio started hanging out more and more with his brother, JR, and his friends. He and his brother were the same size, and though his brother was older, it wasn't hard to convince his friends that Nectorio was close to the same age. Sometimes they'd even convince the girls they met that they were twins just so Nectorio would have a chance with them. One of his brother's friends, Jasmine, had a friend that Nectorio thought was amazing. She was tall like him and had a hot body and a perfect smile. Her name was Alicia, and she was a freshman in high school and Nectorio's first real crush.

Nectorio and JR had met Jasmine and Alicia at the dollar movies, where they would always go when they needed something cheap and entertaining to do. They started going to the movies together after that, just the four of them. Nectorio loved sitting next to Alicia and hardly ever paid attention to what was happening on the screen because he couldn't keep his eyes or his mind off of her. He could tell that she liked him too by the way she would look at him. He hoped she'd never find out that he was in sixth grade, since she was fifteen years old and in ninth grade. They started holding hands during the movies and quickly advanced to making out in the back of the movie theater, which

DJ Necterr

was a little awkward with his brother and Jasmine somewhere in front of them.

Alicia was really sweet when they were together, but Nectorio always felt as though she had a whole different life that he would never really be part of. She was in high school, so he never saw her during school. When he tried to call her just so he could hear her voice a few times late at night, she'd never answer.

One night, after the movies, Jasmine and JR suggested that they go over to Jasmine's house. Her parents were out of town for the weekend, and they could watch movies all night if they wanted to. Nectorio was excited for the chance to be somewhere with Alicia where they wouldn't be surrounded by a bunch of other people. When they got to Jasmine's, JR quickly claimed the upstairs and told Nectorio to stay downstairs with Alicia. They flipped on the TV and turned off the lights. With Larry King blaring in the background, Nectorio had sex for the first time.

He figured it hadn't been Alicia's first time; she seemed pretty experienced. Nectorio really liked Alicia, even though he didn't know her that well. After that first time, they started searching for places to be alone and making up lies for their friends and parents so they could have more time together. Nectorio had to be careful to keep Alicia away from his friends and other people who knew him; he didn't want her to discover how old he really was. They were growing closer and closer, and he could tell that Alicia was starting to really like him.

His fling with Alicia came to an end when she spotted him at a middle school basketball game. She was there with her parents, apparently to watch a cousin who was playing on the opposing team. When Nectorio scored the game-winning basket, all he could hear was people screaming his name. On his way off the court, he spotted her standing on the sidelines, hands on her hips and a look of shock on her face. His teammates rushed him forward toward the locker room before he could say a word to her, and that was the last time he saw her. Another loss in his life, but he convinced himself that she was just some stupid, easy girl, and there were millions more he could be with. That made it hurt a little less. Before long, he and his brother were at it again, and they were lying about his age to a couple of new girls.

Nectorio also joined his first street gang in sixth grade. He had been hearing about the gang for a while and knew it was what he wanted to do. The gang was made up of Mexican kids that were his age, some of the older kids in his school, and a few kids from the high school who were really in charge.

In order to join, he had to get jumped after school. When the bell rang signaling the end of the school day, one of the leaders met him outside of his classroom and led him to the bathroom. When he walked in, he immediately saw that there were about twelve other gang members there waiting for him. His heart raced wildly as they shoved him into the middle of an informal circle. He then had to prove himself by fighting eight of the guys for about twenty seconds. He did his best to defend himself as the punches came flying at him from every direction. He knew he wanted to be part of this group, but he didn't want to be all beaten up and bruised when he went home. That would be too hard to explain.

When it was all over, his head was spinning. He had taken a few really hard hits. He opened his eyes to find the leaders of the gang smiling at him. He had done it, and now he was part of their group. They welcomed him to his new family, and he tried to block out any thoughts of his old one. He felt his right eye beginning to swell and knew he'd have to come up with a good story for his parents, who would notice right away. He didn't like lying to them, but they wouldn't approve of his joining a gang, and there was no way he wanted them to watch him even more closely, so he would come up with a good story. After all, kids his age got in fights all the time, didn't they?

He got home at around ten, four hours later than usual, and they were waiting for him. Unfortunately, his brother wasn't around; he'd hoped JR would be there to help him defend himself. His mom gasped in shock when she saw him, and he figured his eye must look worse than he thought. He knew his bottom lip had also been split open because he could still taste the blood.

His dad didn't even start by asking questions; he just started screaming at him. His basketball coach had called. Why had he skipped practice? Why was he ruining his life? Why didn't he appreciate his family?

Nectorio felt nothing but anger. How dare his father scream at him like that? Didn't his dad know what he had been through and how hard it was to get past the memories and the pain? How hard it was to fit in and to be someone at his school when he had lost his best friend?

His mom went to the kitchen for a cloth for his face while his dad glared at him. He picked up a piece of paper from the coffee table and started waving it in the air like a maniac. It was his progress report, and the worst one ever. His grades had fallen drastically, and he was failing four out of seven classes. Nectorio tried to block out the sound of his dad screaming, but this only made his mother's sobs from the kitchen audible.

"I don't know what to do with you," was the last thing his father said as he picked up his coat and stormed out of the house. His mom came out then with a cold cloth and gently caressed his bruised eye. She gave him a hug and begged him to talk to her as the tears continued to fall slowly from her eyes. Her kindness made him want to tell her everything for a second, but he couldn't. He had to be strong now. He had a new life and a new family, and he didn't want to act like a weak little kid.

"There's nothing to say, Mom," he answered, and he broke free from her embrace and headed for his bedroom. There he put on his headphones and turned up the music as loud as it would go. He stared at the ceiling for hours, until he finally drifted off to sleep.

That first fight began a string of many between Nectorio and his parents, and he started spending more and more time away from home, just to avoid the drama. As part of the gang, he was now not only smoking cigarettes, but smoking weed on a daily basis too. He loved the feeling of being high. He wasn't afraid to do anything, he felt happy, and he never felt sick afterwards.

As a member of the gang, he felt as though he finally belonged and was part of something. It was a status symbol at school, and kids knew not to mess with them. They basically ruled the school, bullying anyone who looked weak or different or looked at them the wrong way. They would take what they wanted from those kids, whether it was lunch money, homework, or a nice bike that they could use or resell. Nectorio always felt slightly bad about stealing from them, but he suppressed those feelings. He had to be tough.

Life at home and school kept getting harder and harder. His parents were getting more and more concerned with his falling grades and the things that were going on at school. Because he was so good at hiding what he'd been doing outside of school, they were starting to wonder if the school was treating him unfairly.

In school, he had to maintain his tough personality, and he was the class clown in every class. He felt that his classes were a waste of time, so he had to find ways to make them interesting for him, and for everyone else. He thought most of the activities and assignments were a joke, and he didn't keep those thoughts to himself. He got into fights often, not only with other students, but also with his teachers. None of them understood him, and because it was obvious that he was in a gang, they all prejudged him. Nobody knew who he really was, and he was okay with that.

Failing grades and fights led to suspension after suspension. Nectorio's parents came to his defense a few times, but after the third suspension, the school and his parents had had enough. A meeting was called to determine what should be done, and Nectorio sat in a room with his principals, his counselors, and his parents. He felt bad when he looked over at his dad, who had dark circles under his eyes and seemed to have more wrinkles than he had a few months earlier. His mom's eyes were puffy, as if she'd been crying or hadn't slept in a week. The administrator explained the situation to everyone in the room, and then looked at Nectorio and asked him why he was having such a hard time in school.

"We're all here to help you, if you'll let us," said the little blonde guidance counselor with a timid smile. He thought about how he'd like a few minutes alone with her and smiled to himself.

"Is something funny?" the principal asked. Nectorio looked down at the floor and said nothing. They wouldn't understand. After what seemed like hours, they couldn't agree on whether the problem was really Nectorio or the school. They finally determined that since he wasn't willing to talk and things hadn't improved after several chances, he would be expelled and would need to attend a different school.

Nectorio's parents seemed almost relieved on the way home, and his dad went on and on about how this would be a fresh start for him. All Nectorio could think about was how awful it would be to have to start over and prove himself again. He would have to leave his gang and his friends and try to fit in somewhere completely new. He smiled and nodded at his dad, figuring he might as well let them have their moment of happiness and peace.

The moment didn't last, though, because in order to survive and fit in at his new school Nectorio had to be even tougher. He continued to get failing grades, fight anyone who got in his way, and disrupt his classes. He lasted only a few months at his new school, until the brilliant decision was made that he should be home-schooled.

Home-schooling was a joke. With no structured schedule, Nectorio had lots of spare time on his hands. Instead of using that time to do anything constructive, he found ways to hook up with his old friends. He started drinking and smoking even more, and getting into more trouble.

Nectorio was in eighth grade when he realized that it was too hard to get around, and he decided to steal his parents' car for the first time. He waited until they were asleep, then quietly snuck the keys out of his mom's purse and crept into the garage. He started it up and backed out quickly, watching carefully for a light to come on in the house, but it never did. It was five a.m. when he rolled back in, still slightly high. He smiled to himself as he slid the keys back into her purse and headed for his bedroom. It would be much easier to stay in touch with the old gang and make new and better friends now that he had a way to get around.

Nectorio's relationship with his parents continued to disintegrate. It seemed like all they ever did was fight. He came home late almost every night, and sometimes not at all, if he was too busy with a girl or the gang, or just not in the mood to deal with them. He got caught with the car a few times, and his dad tried to ground him, which never worked. The third time he got caught, they threatened to call the police if it happened again. Then they gave up, for good it seemed.

Though Nectorio felt relieved, he also felt sad and angry. His parents began to focus all their attention on his siblings rather than on what was happening with him. His sister had just graduated and started college, so they were nervous and excited about that. JR was playing for the varsity baseball team, a sports star not only at school, but also at home. Everyone was doing great, it seemed, except for him. His life was spiraling out of control and he wasn't quite sure how to feel about it.

Chapter 5
A Young Boss in Training

Nectorio ended up back in public school his freshman year. He had done okay with his home-schooling toward the end of eighth grade. He had learned how to barely get by with his grades and still have fun with his friends. He did his best to hide his activities with girls, the gang, and his older friends from his parents, and they believed, probably because they wanted to believe it so badly, that he was doing much better. Nectorio started to harass them about going back to school. He told them that he thought he could do even better there, and that he was ready to get back into sports. School was where most kids were during the day, and he knew there were lots of opportunities there. They decided, with a lot of prodding from him, that he might be ready to go back.

Though Nectorio was glad to be back in school where the action and lots of the people his age were, school itself was just as ridiculous as ever. He had to start all over with the game of trying to fit in, and though he knew a few kids from before, he was basically the new kid all over again. He was judged by his appearance, and he had the feeling that some of his teachers had already discussed his school records, probably in the teacher's lounge in front of teachers he didn't even have yet.

To cope with the adjustment, Nectorio quickly resumed his role as class clown, not only so he could be cool and make new friends, but also to keep himself from being bored to death. Once again, he had a hard time getting along with his teachers, who all looked at him and only saw what they wanted to see—a troublemaker. They all seemed more concerned with being on a power trip than truly teaching anything. One teacher, Mr. Jensen, who taught ninth grade composition, was the only one who seemed to treat him fairly and even take an interest in him. He'd stand outside his door every day and greet the students on their way in. Nectorio was amazed at how quickly he had learned all their names. It only took him two days, while Nectorio figured he'd never know all the names of the kids in class. While Mr. J said hi to everyone at the door, he always had a conversation with Nectorio for a few minutes. It didn't seem fake, and it didn't feel like he was being judged, so Nectorio decided he liked him. They talked about hobbies and favorite movies. To Nectorio's surprise, it turned out they even liked some of the same music.

Outside of school, Nectorio started to really focus on his music. He had started his own mini-business doing what he loved: working as a DJ. He started out by DJing for some friends at small birthday parties mostly for free. The first time he did it, he realized it was something he could do twenty-four hours a day and never get bored. He loved the music and the way he could play exactly what they wanted to hear, always keeping the crowd dancing, screaming, and happy. Then it was on to bigger house parties for some of his older friends, and friends of their friends. Soon he was actually getting paid to do what he loved.

Before Nectorio knew it, the school was starting to use him for his talents. He became known as the school DJ. He wasn't making much money, but he was doing what he absolutely loved, and word got out quickly that he was really good at it. The school hired him to do school dances and basketball games. It was cheaper for them to hire an existing student, and everyone knew that he would do a great job.

Nectorio got caught up in a whirlwind of excitement as his reputation as a DJ continued to grow. He soon found himself working in the clubs. Even though they were eighteen and older clubs, he found connections through his brother and his older friends and had the opportunity to prove himself. He absolutely loved working the clubs where everyone was older and just out to have a good time. Everyone was dressed up and looking their best, and he loved watching the crowd grow as the night went on. The faster he could make the excitement and volume escalate, the happier he was. He often worked weeknights, and even when he got home in the early morning, he couldn't go right to sleep. He was too excited and filled with adrenaline from his night's work, so he always stayed up a few hours more before drifting off to sleep.

Getting up for school began to get harder and harder. When he finally did get up, it was too late and too much of a hassle to get ready and go, so his attendance started to suffer right along with his grades. When he did go to school, Mr. Jensen started asking lots of questions about where he'd been, or what was going on with him. He knew the guy was probably just concerned about him, but it was really none of his business, so he didn't say much to him. His class was one of the only ones that Nectorio wasn't failing. One of the major grades in the class was for journaling about a topic on the board, or any topic the students wanted. Nectorio always wrote about his music and even started to write some lyrics of his own. Mr. Jensen always gave him full credit and wrote positive comments on his papers.

As his reputation as a DJ grew and his grades and attendance plummeted, Nectorio unconsciously decided it was just easier to not be in school where he always ended up bored or in trouble. He started ditching the classes he hated the most with his older friends and hanging out with them at their houses. He felt as if he had always fit in better with them; kids his age were so immature. They'd pick a different house every day and smoke weed and play with their turntables, laughing at all those kids who were sitting through chemistry and trigonometry while they were having a great time.

At age sixteen, Nectorio, having barely made it into eleventh grade, was placed in a continuation school. The school was meant for students with bad attendance and was structured differently than regular public school to keep the students interested and there.

Nectorio was still drinking, smoking, and doing pretty much whatever he wanted. Adrian was one of his better friends who lived in his neighborhood. He was one of the guys who had jumped him into the street gang back in sixth grade. Adrian looked much different now, though; he had grown in size and was much bigger than he had been back then. It was obvious that he had been lifting weights since the sixth grade. Adrian was the friend who got Nectorio his first pound of weed, and indirectly changed his life drastically.

Nectorio quickly realized that the drug would be great to have not only for his own personal use, but also for business use. If he could start buying and selling weed and combined the money from those sales with his money from DJing, he could be rich before even graduating from high school. With money, he wouldn't have to worry about fitting in anymore and he'd be able to buy whatever he wanted for his friends, family, and himself.

In order to actually make his business work, though, Nectorio knew he needed more money. He had to have the funds to buy his supply, and he wasn't making enough on his own. He started to steal from other students at school, promising himself that he'd only do this until the business got going, then never again. He knew deep down that he was a good person and no thief; he just needed to get things started.

Nectorio learned to watch carefully for the right opportunities at school. If there was a group activity in a class, he'd wait until all the groups were busy talking and pretending to work, and then he'd go through backpacks that they'd carelessly left lying around. Once he got used to it, he mastered the art of being sneaky. In phys ed, he'd pretend to be looking for something in his backpack, then quickly and sneakily go through whatever he could find. When someone would complain about money being stolen from a backpack, he'd join right in and talk about how that was bullshit, and the school needed better security. Nobody ever seemed to suspect him, and he never got caught.

Once, Nectorio even went for two months without eating lunch at school so he could rob other students. He finally gathered up enough money to purchase more drugs for himself and his new business. The more money he came up with, the more he seemed to want or need. His business was picking up, and he wanted it to keep growing. Within about four months, he had a reputation and had become the "flossy" type.

With the help of his parents, who felt he was finally doing a little better in school, he got a car. It was a nice-looking shiny black Mercedes Benz. He started wearing new clothes to school and piling on more and more jewelry to show off. He was a sixteen-year-old driving a Benz to school and always had a pocket full of money. It didn't take long for the kids in his school and soon his whole district to figure out that he was the weed man. Nectorio became the marijuana supplier to every interested kid in the school district, and even some older kids who had heard about him. He was making money faster than he could spend it, and along with that money came more fun and more friends. He was never really quite sure which friends were true friends and which were there for the money, but he decided to just enjoy his success as long as he had it.

Being new and having no guidance in the business, it didn't take Nectorio long to get caught. About eight months into the business, he ran into his first snitch. Jose was in the same grade and Nectorio knew him, but not as well as he thought. He wasn't someone he spent a lot of time with, but he did hang out with him occasionally, and he never dreamed that Jose would alter his life so drastically.

They were hanging out at a party one night, and Jose started asking questions. He wanted to know how Nectorio got started and how the business actually worked. The questions seemed innocent enough, and Jose seemed harmless, so Nectorio told him how it all worked. They were both high, and it seemed like small talk to Nectorio. It was the first big mistake Nectorio had made.

Jose knew that Nectorio always kept his sacks in a female classmate's purse. On a rainy Tuesday morning, Jose tried to steal that purse and ran out of algebra class with it. He got caught with it immediately, and when the drugs were found and he was questioned by the police, he told them that they belonged to Nectorio. The investigation was short, and Nectorio knew that lying wouldn't do him much good; everyone in the district pretty much knew about his business. He was arrested and went to jail.

Nectorio felt like his world was crumbling when he was arrested, but he tried not to show it. In his mind, he really hadn't done anything wrong. He had only been trying to make money to share with himself, his family, and his friends. His motives weren't selfish, and he knew he was good at what he did. His biggest fear was how his parents would react, and if he would be able to get back to business and DJing when he got out. He wasn't sure if time in jail would hurt or help his reputation as both a dealer and a DJ.

His trip to jail was surreal. He sat in the back of the squad car quietly, trying to tune out the officers that were chatting in the front seat like it was just any ordinary day. He realized then that, for them, it was just another day. They pulled into a compound surrounded by towers and gated off from the rest of the world, and he watched the officer punch in a code to electronically open the gate to his new home.

One of the officers opened his door and grabbed his arm, pulling him roughly from the police car. It pissed him off a little, but he knew he was probably in no position to complain, so he kept his mouth shut. They led him to the intake hallway and he took a deep breath, knowing this was not going to be fun at all and wishing he was at home, at a club, even at school. Anywhere but where he was. He wondered what Mr. Jensen was doing at that moment, and smiled to himself as he thought about what a great journal writing topic this would be. An intake officer gave him a dirty look when he caught him smiling, and he quickly returned to his original stone face, the one that he would wear his entire time in that place.

At intake, they removed his handcuffs and then made him take off his shoes, his belt, and all of his jewelry. He had to empty his pockets, which was no big deal really; he only had some spare change and his wallet, which he never kept much money in. He did have pictures of his sisters and brother in there, though, and one of his parents if he remembered correctly. He surrendered it, hoping that he'd get it back in the same condition.

Nectorio started to really feel like a criminal when an officer patted him down for the first time. It was a terribly uncomfortable feeling, being in that room with a bunch of strangers who looked at him like they hated him and having some guy groping at him like an idiot. These people didn't know him, and they never would. He was guided, actually almost pushed, to the metal detector, where it seemed he passed the test. Apparently he didn't have anything he shouldn't or couldn't.

Next, he had to help some older woman who looked like she hated life and hadn't slept in a week with paperwork. He gave minimal answers to every question, not wanting to share his story with her, or anyone, for that matter. Another straight-faced officer led him into the showering area, where he was given soap, shampoo, and towels through a two-way door. He stood in the shower letting the semi-hot water rain down on him and cursing himself for telling Jose anything. Next time, he'd have to be much smarter about who his real friends were. He decided sadly that he'd probably only ever had one true friend—Richard.

After his shower, they gave him his new clothing—socks, a T-shirt, sweatpants, a sweatshirt, even underwear. He felt his identity being stripped away and assumed he'd look a lot like everyone else there when he emerged from the shower area.

Next, Nectorio was led to his cell, which was in a block of cells called Pod B. It was cold and dark and had built-in bunks, a desk with a wooden stool, a sink, and a toilet. It appeared that nobody else was housed in that cell at that time, and for a brief moment, Nectorio felt a little lucky.

Nectorio's first few nights in jail were terrifying. He tried to act tough and hide his fear, but it was a miserable place to be. His cell was cold and dark, and all he had was a board with a paper-thin mattress to sleep on. He missed his house, his parents, and his bedroom more than he ever thought he could. He started to wish he'd spent more time there when he had the opportunity.

Every guy in jail with him looked angry and mean, and he figured they were all trying to hide the same fears and regrets that he was. He wasn't taking any chances though, so he didn't even try to talk to any of them for the first month. He just focused on settling into his new life, staying out of trouble and dreaming of the day he would get out.

His life became a monotonous routine of mealtimes, classes, and a daily shower. He got used to the fact that he was always being watched, and eventually it only really bothered him during visiting hours. He figured it was pretty sad that the highlight of his day was a shower.

DJ Necterr

Nectorio was a small guy at the time, and everyone else was bigger than him, so it became the game of the other inmates to test him. He'd gotten pushed around a little, and a few of the guys seemed threatened by him and tried to start fights. Nectorio just walked away when he could; he figured a fight might extend his stay, and that was something he definitely didn't want.

The meals were disgusting, and Nectorio had a problem eating dairy. He could never really explain it, but it was a mental rather than a medical problem. Any time a meal with dairy in it came, he would skip dinner, which only made him feel weaker and smaller.

Nectorio's father was disappointed in him and rarely visited. His mother was worried about him, and each time he saw her she looked older and more stressed. He tried not to imagine her coming through the gates and being patted down just so she could visit her son. Under video and audio surveillance with an armed guard nearby, she filled him in about his siblings, who were off excelling at what they did. He always knew when the end of a visit was near because her eyes would fill with tears, and she would quickly hug him and rush out of the room. Nectorio hadn't meant to hurt her; he had only been trying to make all of their lives better, and he vowed never to get caught again once he got out.

Chapter 6
Reunion

Nectorio spent his whole senior year of school in jail. He tried not to think about the fact that other people his age were hanging out, going to parties and the prom. He knew many of them would be busy planning their futures while his felt like it was on hold. Most of the time, he wasn't really sure how he felt about any of it. A mixture of emotions was always swirling around inside him. Anger, bitterness, fear, sadness, and guilt for disappointing his parents all fought for control of him.

There was one other feeling that he tried desperately to cling to, and that was determination. Nectorio resolved that no matter what he ended up doing when he got out, he would never find himself in a position like this again. Whenever he had the chance he reminded himself of it by telling himself or writing it down either in his journal or as part of a song he was working on.

His life in jail continued as a monotonous series of seemingly endless days. Every day he would be awakened at five a.m., then go to breakfast at six. After breakfast, it was back to his cell. It hadn't taken him long to figure out that the unused bunk in his cell would remain empty. This was something he had been grateful for at first, but as the days wore on, he began to wish he had a cellmate. Even if the guy was an idiot, he'd at least be someone to talk to. Nectorio was isolated from the general population because of his age, so he spent most of his time alone in his cell. He quickly learned that it was harder than he had ever imagined it would be to be alone all of the time.

He participated in the mandatory juvenile school program, which was an endless cycle of classes and physical education with other inmates who were high schoolers. Of course, everyone there was trying to maintain a tough image, so the other inmates were not outgoing or friendly. It always felt like a fight was about to break out, so Nectorio was careful not to make eye contact with any of them. He thought the whole scene was pretty ridiculous since they were all just scared and angry kids like he was. If they would just talk to each other, they'd all figure that out in a hurry, and the time might go by a little faster. Nectorio tried to let himself enjoy the phys ed classes each day, reminiscing about the old days when he excelled in sports and everyone admired him. He loved being able to expend some energy and play again, but purposely hid some of his talent, afraid that if he appeared to be too good at anything, he might cause a fight.

There were no teachers like Mr. Jensen here. These teachers didn't appear to be motivated by a desire to inspire their students. They looked at Nectorio and the others as though they were all just losers who would never amount to anything in life. They were clearly there to collect a paycheck and did not believe that any of their students could or would succeed in class or at anything, for that matter. They were all business, and never smiled. It seemed like they were afraid that if they smiled, something horrible might happen to them. Nectorio also had the feeling that they kept the academic expectations low because they were slightly afraid of their students. It was a horrible feeling, to have people who didn't even know him fear him.

Nectorio did what he had to in order to get passing grades. He didn't want to have to deal with school when he got out, and he didn't want to do anything that might hinder his getting out on time. Instead of acting the way he used to in school, he was quiet and obedient. He figured there really wasn't anyone he needed to impress in here. He kept to himself and daydreamed through monotone lessons, then quietly completed his assignments and turned them in. He often finished the work first—it was really simple—and he'd spend the rest of the work time writing in his journal or scribbling down song lyrics on scrap paper. He journaled for himself and for Mr. Jensen, even though he knew his old teacher had probably forgotten all about him and would never see it.

Lunch and dinner were at the same time every day, and Nectorio was sure the food got worse as the days went by. He pretty much kept to himself during mealtimes too. He was very intimidated, as he was caught between the juvenile and adult system. He was a small kid constantly surrounded by grown men, all of whom were criminals and many of whom liked to entertain themselves by bullying. After dinner, it was shower time, then back to his cell.

Because Nectorio was isolated, he had no television privileges. This was a pretty big deal because TV would have been a great distraction. He devoted more and more time to writing his music and poetry, which he later decided probably saved him from going completely crazy in that tiny dark cell.

Most days he wasn't even sure what day of the week it was until his mom visited and told him. He tried to keep track of the days and weeks on a notepad, so he could cross them off one by one as he got closer to his release date. One particular day started off strangely, and Nectorio knew that something was wrong. The atmosphere, which was always dark and depressing, had gotten even gloomier. The guards were more sinister, and unusually quiet, and looked completely distracted and defeated. A few of them even looked like they'd been crying, which was definitely a red flag since they were grown men who always looked and acted extremely tough.

The next day was the same, and the inmates started talking amongst themselves about what could possibly be going on. They were suddenly not allowed to watch the news or have newspapers, which Nectorio later found out was a precaution to prevent riots. He felt extremely isolated and helpless. For all he knew the world was ending out there, and he was trapped inside with no information, and there was absolutely nothing he could do about it.

His mother showed up for a visit the next day, and to his surprise, his dad was with her. He knew for sure that something was up when his dad showed up again; he usually only came every other week, and Nectorio was sure he had been there the previous week. He noticed something was wrong immediately by the way they walked and the sadder than usual looks on their faces.

His parents told him about what had happened two days earlier, on September 11. They let him know that they were instructed not to tell him anything about the attacks, as he assumed all visitors that week were told. They explained what had happened in great detail anyway. He sat in shocked silence, trying to control his mixed emotions of anger and sadness as his father quietly described the planes, the crumbling towers with people diving out of the windows, the heroes who risked and lost their lives, and the missing persons posters that covered the devastated city as the world watched in helpless shock and anger.

The guard who was supposed to be listening and watching closely didn't appear to notice or care what was going on. He was probably thinking about the same images that Nectorio was now hearing about. His mother sat quietly next to his father, nodding and dabbing at her eyes with a tissue. He got the feeling she'd cried many times during that week and felt bad that there was nothing he could do to make her feel better, or to protect them if something like that would happen in their city.

When they left, his dad told Nectorio that he loved him and actually hugged him. Nectorio couldn't remember the last time his dad had hugged him. He seemed grateful again for his son, and for the fact that he was alive and safe when so many other parents were now searching for their sons and daughters.

When they left that day, Nectorio was filled with nervous and angry energy. He started to work out in his cell, and thus began a series of tough workouts including hundreds of sit-ups and push-ups. He pushed himself until he was physically exhausted and the pain was unbearable. These workouts became part of a daily ritual for him which eventually caused him to gain forty-five pounds. He had gone into jail as a scrawny boy but vowed to come out a muscular man. He also knew that his physical appearance could either greatly help or hinder him during his stay, and with nothing but time on his hands, he figured he might as well use it to improve and possibly protect himself.

Nectorio found that the more he tried to control the anger that often overcame him by working out, the angrier he got. He was angry at the world. The old anger and bitterness at King for taking away his best friend and his childhood had come back stronger. He was angry at whoever had orchestrated the attacks on his country, angry at himself, and angry at the snitch who had put him in that horrible place. He worked hard to channel that anger into his workouts and to focus on his writing, afraid that if he didn't, he might kill someone who looked at him the wrong way at the dinner table.

Holidays came and went one by one, and he spent Thanksgiving, Christmas, and New Year's incarcerated all because of a snitch. In jail, the holidays were no different than any other day. Sometimes the cooks would make a meal slightly different by adding a side dish or a special dessert, as if more nasty food might somehow make them forget that their families and friends were all somewhere celebrating the holidays together. There was one minor change on New Year's Eve. They took down every clock in the place so that there wouldn't be any incidents at midnight. It definitely went down as Nectorio's worst New Year's Eve ever, and he promised himself the next one would be different.

His parents tried to do little things to make the holidays brighter by visiting more frequently. They brought him cookies or small gifts that were on the list of acceptable items for him to receive, all inspected by nosy guards. They'd spend the time with him telling him what was going on at home, in the city, and in the world. They talked a lot about his siblings, and he watched his dad's eyes fill with pride as he talked about how well they were all doing. It reminded him of the days when his dad had looked at him like that after a big game or a great report card. Those days were long gone, though, and any brightness they brought with them left when they did, making it even harder to accept the harsh reality he was living.

The new year started out with Nectorio realizing that the snitch had done him a favor. If he hadn't been sitting in jail because of Jose, he wouldn't have met who he met next. Nectorio was standing in the lunch line waiting quietly for it to move and wondering what kind of slop they'd pile onto his plate that day. Suddenly, someone slammed into him from behind, pushing him into the guy in front of him. That guy then lost his balance and it was a domino effect. A fight broke out behind him, and he quickly tried to move forward, not wanting the guards to think he was involved. The guards were on top of the chaos behind him within minutes, yelling and swearing as they pounded on them with their sticks.

The guys in front of him were trying to figure out who had pushed them, and he figured a fight would break out there any second too. All he wanted to do was stay out of it; he didn't need any trouble so close to his release date.

Suddenly a big guy came rushing at him, and Nectorio braced himself. He didn't want to fight, but he wasn't going to run either. He hadn't done anything wrong. Ready to throw the first punch, he looked up into the eyes of a slightly familiar face, and noticed that the guy was smiling down at him. Nectorio thought the guy had looked familiar when he saw him from afar at dinner a few times, but he never tried to pursue anything since his goal was always to keep to himself as much as possible.

It took a moment for it to register that Nectorio was looking at Eddie Hernandez. Eddie told the guys in front of them who were ready to brawl that everything was fine, and that Nectorio was an old friend of his. They backed off and refocused on waiting for the line to move as Eddie and Nectorio began to reconnect. Eddie was exactly the same as he had always been. He was very outgoing and funny and acted like he and Nectorio were the best of friends.

Eddie was his old best friend's older brother, a member of the family that Nectorio had felt a part of so long ago. Nectorio was actually sitting in the same jail as Richard's brother. Eddie was in jail for pretty much the same reason as Nectorio, and he quietly told him about the family business as they pretended to eat their disgusting lunchtime meals under close watch of the guards. Eddie quickly told him how his older brother, Jerome, had a booming business. Nectorio listened cautiously and tried not to say too much. Although Eddie was like long-lost family to him, he had learned a very important lesson, and that was to trust nobody.

As Eddie bragged about the business, Nectorio wondered about Richard. He waited awhile to ask, and was sad to hear that while Eddie and Jerome were doing pretty well working together, Richard was another story. He had distanced himself from everyone, and they really didn't even talk to him anymore. Nobody really knew how or what he was doing, and that was apparently how he wanted things to be.

Eddie and Nectorio tried to connect at mealtimes every day during his last few weeks in jail. It helped a little to know somebody in that horrible place, and to have someone familiar to talk to. Eddie had a few friends in there too, and they immediately accepted Nectorio when Eddie introduced him first as a friend, and soon afterwards as a brother.

The days went by more quickly now that Nectorio had finally figured out how to fill them.

Knowing that the end of his sentence was near helped too. He was able to focus more in his classes, and he actually tried to do well rather than just get by. He had his workouts, which were starting to really pay off; he looked and felt better physically than he ever had. He filled any other time he had with his writing, which he strongly believed was good and getting better. He only wished he had someone like Mr. Jensen to share it with, who could confirm that it really was good. Now he also had some friends, or at least people to talk to, on the inside. Life wasn't good, but it was getting better, and his release date was quickly approaching.

Eddie talked to his older brother, Jerome, every day, and Jerome was excited to hear that Eddie had found Nectorio. By that time, Eddie knew exactly why Nectorio was there, and that he would be getting out soon. He had shared all of that information with Jerome. One day, Eddie told Nectorio that Jerome wanted to include him in the family business. Eddie was going to be serving time long after Nectorio got out, and Jerome needed someone to replace him until then. Before Nectorio even knew what was happening, a plan was put in place for Jerome to pick him up at the jail as soon as he got out.

Nectorio was not sure about going back into business at that time. He knew he was sitting in jail for the same thing he was considering going back into. He felt like his life might be passing him by.

He had disappointed a lot of people, especially his parents, and he felt bad about that. He weighed the pros and cons of getting mixed up with Jerome and Eddie carefully in his head for days.

He thought about his options during his workouts and started making lists in his journal of the things he could possibly do when he got out. There were two things he absolutely knew he had to do. He had to get back to his music, and he wanted to find Richard. He knew that he was talented and could make a life for himself and his family using his talents. He wanted to be able to focus completely on his music when he got out, but he worried that it would take time and money to re-establish himself.

He realized that his biggest concern had become meeting up once again with his old best friend, Richard—or Richie, as they called him at that time. He wanted to make sure that Richie was okay, and he had a feeling that everything would be like when they were kids. They had the kind of friendship that would stand the test of time. Nectorio knew in his gut that even though he hadn't seen Richie for years, it would be as if they had never been apart. He also had a nagging feeling that something might be wrong. Richie was secluded and wanted nothing to do with anyone, and Nectorio just knew that if he could get him to talk to him, he'd be able to find out was going on and help him.

DJ Necterr

He knew he couldn't make contact with him from jail, but once he was out, if he was working with Richard's brothers, they'd surely reconnect eventually. Even if they didn't know where he was now, they were bound to make contact with him. The other benefit would be that if things went well, he'd have easy money again. He knew he was good at dealing, and it wouldn't take long for him to make enough cash to get on his feet again. He'd be able to get back to his DJ business too. Once those three things happened, he could decide for himself whether to stay in the business or to try to make it doing what he loved as a DJ. No matter what, he knew he would be much more careful this time; he had learned his lesson.

The Perfect Gangster

DJ Necterr

Chapter 7
Back to Business

On January 8, 2002, Nectorio was released from prison. He was escorted out to a holding area, where the same unfriendly woman who had checked him in many months ago processed his release paperwork with the same unenthusiastic motions. He didn't realize how trapped he had felt on the inside until he stepped out into the crisp winter air. It felt good to be free again, and he remembered his vow to himself to stay that way as he waited for his ride.

His mom and dad picked him up and were so happy and relieved to see their son. They quickly noticed that he had gone from a sixteen-year-old boy to an eighteen-year-old man while he was locked up. He was relieved that the anger and disappointment he thought they had toward him appeared to be gone. His mother had a sparkle in her eyes again as she chattered on and on about some remodeling projects they had done while he was gone. His dad seemed happy too, probably to be picking up his son rather than just coming to that dreadful place to visit him. He hoped that maybe their relationship could return to normal now, and he would be someone they could talk to and about with pride again like they had in the past and like they did now about his siblings.

Nectorio was released on house arrest with the stipulation that he could not leave his house for thirty days. Though he wasn't thrilled about being on house arrest, he knew anything would be better than the life he'd been living for almost a year. He was eighteen years old and ready to start all over again. He was stronger and smarter now, and he had come up with some great ideas for how he could incorporate some of the stuff he'd written in prison into his music when he got his DJ business started again. He felt free and smarter and stronger than ever, and with his whole life in front of him, he couldn't help but be excited.

His homecoming was pleasantly quiet, and he was okay with that. His brother was in the south playing baseball, and his sister was still in college. His older sister had a family of her own now and was wrapped up in her own life. His mother had shared pictures and stories with him while he was in jail, so he didn't need many updates. It was fine this way; he didn't want anyone making a big deal about his getting out, or about his being in jail in the first place.

Nectorio quickly noticed how different life was as an eighteen year old. He was an adult and felt like all of the parental rules had been lifted. Even though he couldn't leave the house, life was so much better. He could eat what he wanted and sleep whenever and however much he wanted. He could listen to the music he wanted to at any hour of the day or night. He appreciated his new life as a free man and as an adult. It was easy for him to notice now all of the seemingly ordinary pleasures he had missed while he was in jail.

He felt really good about things, and only slightly afraid occasionally of the new responsibilities that he thought might come with being an adult. He knew he would now be totally responsible for taking care of himself. He thought he might have to do what he knew how to do best without getting caught at least for a while. He was physically stronger than he had ever been in his life, and he knew mentally he was much smarter also. He felt invincible.

On his very first day out, Jerome, the older brother of Eddie and Richie, met him at his house. Jerome wanted to talk business right away. Nectorio secretly wished he would have given him a little time to get his thoughts straight and adjust to being out. He would never say that to Jerome, though; he didn't want him to think he was scared or couldn't be trusted.

Jerome's plan was to take over the streets and the jails with the drug trade. Jerome explained that he had the streets pretty well taken care of, but he wanted help with the jails. Jerome told him that they could charge almost triple on the inside what they could get for the same thing on the street. Since Nectorio had just gotten out, Jerome thought he was perfect for the job because he knew how things worked and was familiar with some of the inmates and the guards.

To Nectorio's surprise, Jerome asked him if he could figure out a way to go back to jail soon to get a system put into place there. Nectorio hesitated. He wasn't sure he wanted to do that. He had just done almost a year in prison, and although it had taught him a lot, he wasn't in a hurry to go back. He had been locked away like an animal for all of that time, and the thought of being caged up again made him sick. Besides, he was making plans to do things right this time. He knew he had the skill and talent to make it as a DJ doing what he loved.

Nectorio decided he hated the plan and didn't even want to consider doing it. He struggled with the idea internally, though, because he realized that he needed to be able to support himself now that he was an adult. He had no intention of continuing to live with his parents as an adult, so he needed a plan. He wasn't sure how or when he'd be able to get a job, and realized he didn't even know how he would eat or survive on his own. Jerome explained that the payout was good and the perks were great. Like every good dealer, he was very convincing, and since Nectorio needed a quick way to make some money, he considered doing it.

While he was thinking about Jerome's plan, Nectorio got a call from a girl he had gone out with in high school. Her name was Cookie, and she was incredible. Nectorio couldn't believe that Cookie wasn't with someone else by now, and he was excited to hear from her. She had heard that he was out of jail and wanted to see how he was doing. She said she had really missed him and worried about him while he was gone. Nectorio didn't hesitate to invite her over. He was excited to show her how different he looked. He was no longer a skinny little kid; he was now big and muscular from his jail workouts, which he continued to do at home. He was also a little nervous. He hadn't had the chance to be with or even really talk to a girl for almost a year. He wondered if seeing her would be awkward.

Nectorio was amazed when he answered the door and saw Cookie standing there; she was beautiful. She had always been pretty, but now she looked like a woman. She was slim, but with a great curvy body, honey-brown hair, and light skin. She greeted him with a huge hug and kiss, saying she couldn't believe how different he looked.

There was nothing awkward about her visit. It seemed as if they had never been apart. She was sweet and so much fun to be around; she constantly made him laugh. What he loved most about her, though, was that he never felt like she judged him for anything he had done. She liked him for who he was even though she knew about his past. Most importantly, it seemed like she had waited for him. He decided to spend as much time as possible with her. She would definitely make his time on house arrest more interesting and easy to deal with, and he felt like it was just meant to be.

Cookie spent every day with him. They did ordinary things; hung out, watched TV or movies, and listened to music. She was a great cook and loved to surprise him with a gourmet lunch or dinner that she spent hours planning and preparing. Nectorio shared some of the lyrics and poetry he had written in jail with her, and this made him feel closer to her than ever. He had never wanted to share them with anyone else, and Cookie was so encouraging. She seemed to love his work. He also shared his dream of working as a DJ again with her, and she promised to do whatever she could to help and support him in his pursuit of that dream.

Jerome continued to pressure him for an answer, and it only took Nectorio a few days to decide he needed to work with Jerome, even though he was torn because he was having such a great time with Cookie. Since he was on house arrest, he knew that if he violated, he would have to do thirty days in jail. It was a short enough time that he knew he could easily handle it, but long enough for him to complete the work he needed to do. He came up with a plan to violate. It would be lucrative and exciting, but most of all, it would allow him to become independent. He was a grown man now and falling in love. He didn't want to be living with his parents. He also still had the goal of getting in touch with Richard and knew that the best way to do that would be through Jerome.

Before violating his parole, Nectorio tried to get started DJing again. He quickly realized that the DJ game is like any other type of business. People have to recognize the product to want to get it. Just like the drug game. If a dealer goes away and comes back, he has to prove that he does good work. Nectorio had been gone for almost a year and other DJs had taken his place. His name wasn't as well known or popular as it had once been, and it was difficult for him to get consistent work. It would take some time to build his reputation back up, which didn't really bother him. He knew he would have no problem doing that. The problem was, he needed to be making money now to support himself and to give Cookie the things she deserved. This was just one more good reason for him to get back into the business with Jerome.

Jerome knew it was important to show Nectorio how lucrative his business was and what kind of life he could have. He could also tell that Nectorio was falling in love with Cookie. He set up an all expense paid trip to Miami, where Nectorio and Cookie spent an amazing weekend together.

Jerome made sure they flew first class and had booked a three-night stay for them at the Ritz-Carlton of South Beach. Cookie screamed in delight as she danced around in the luxury suite before he swept her up and carried her to the bedroom. They ate at the most famous and romantic restaurants in the city, and when it was time to pay the bill, Nectorio didn't even have to look at the totals; he just handed over the credit card Jerome had given him to use.

They spend their days on the beautiful beach, Cookie showing off her gorgeous body in a tiny pink bikini, and Nectorio lying proudly beside her. They danced the nights away at some incredible clubs, and being in that environment again only fueled Nectorio's fire for being a DJ even more. He could picture himself doing what these guys were doing, only better. He had to get back to doing what he was meant to do as soon as possible.

When they arrived back at the hotel, they were up all night each night having amazing sex. By the end of the weekend, Nectorio knew that this girl was the love of his life, and after he got things started with Jerome, he was ready to build a great life together with her.

Nectorio didn't tell Cookie about his plan; he didn't want to scare or upset her and ruin the awesome time they were having together. She would find out all too soon, but Nectorio was confident that if she had waited this long for him, she would have no problem waiting another thirty days. Once he got back out of jail this time, he'd have all the money he needed to take care of her and continue to pursue his lifelong dream.

When Nectorio got back home, the authorities were outside his door ready to take him in, just as Nectorio had planned. Cookie watched in shock and despair as they cuffed him and took him away. She knew he had violated his house arrest but had no idea they would be waiting for them. It broke her heart to see how they violently handled him as if he were just some street thug, when he was the man she was in love with. He had told her not to worry before they dragged him away, but she didn't know if she could believe him. She also couldn't bear the thought of not being with him every day.

As soon as he got back to jail and settled in, Nectorio got busy. He had to work quickly and carefully to get the drug trade set up. His first major job was to get to know the guards and figure out which ones were crooked enough to work with. He had to be extremely cautious with this, because if he chose incorrectly, the whole plan would be exposed. He set up work to be handled through a handful of them. The understanding was that they would look the other way on visits and that's how the drugs would make their way inside. Then the guards would get what they wanted in return, as long as everything went as planned. Some of them wanted the discounted drugs as payment, but most wanted cash. It was a great way for them to supplement their income.

Finding buyers was no challenge on the inside. The jail was filled with addicts who would do anything for a fix. They had no support, were surrounded by drugs and other guys doing drugs, and had the addiction. They couldn't just stop because they were in jail, and some of them actually started because they were in jail. What easier way was there to try to deal with their situation and forget why and how they were there in the first place? Most of the guys who had been there for a long time just wanted to find a way to escape reality and forget that life was going on without them outside of the prison walls.

Nectorio's job was to make sure everything ran smoothly on the inside. He was the eyes and ears of Jerome, who would make arrangements on the outside to do the hand-to-hand work and get the families paid. It didn't take them long to have a well-trained team in place.

There were also enforcers who would take care of things in a very violent way if and when things went wrong. Jerome and Nectorio weren't taking any chances. They needed this to work, and neither of them could afford to get caught.

Nectorio was in the general population now instead of being separated like he had been as a juvenile. It was much easier to communicate with other inmates than it had been before. He was in a cell block with about thirty other inmates this time. He was able to pretty much run the place, with the exception of the other races. He knew what he was doing, though, and quickly earned their respect. Just as in school, he had a reputation here. Everyone knew that he could get them what they wanted and needed.

There was also a lot of stress and pressure for Nectorio. If anyone got caught or snitched, he knew that he could face a lot of jail time, and that was something he wasn't interested in doing. He had plans to get out for good this time and build his life and new business with his girl. He knew there were many desperate men all around him just waiting for a chance to reduce a sentence or make a deal. He was extremely careful about who he trusted on the inside and kept all of his relationships on a strict business level.

His time was passing much more quickly this time. He was extremely busy setting up deals and keeping watch for Jerome. He continued with his workouts just as he had before. In what little spare time he did have, he would occasionally write again. He journaled, wrote lyrics, and wrote letters to Cookie. He smiled proudly when she came to visit, and he caught some of the other inmates eyeing him jealously. He was lucky to have her, and she always found a way to make him smile and laugh.

DJ Necterr

His parents didn't visit this time, but that was okay. He would make up for lost time with them when he got out. He figured his going back had probably been especially hard on his mother, and he planned to buy her something really nice to make up for it when he got out. If they could forgive him for the last year, this thirty days shouldn't be too big of a deal for them when he got out again.

Nectorio had a plan, and he knew exactly what he wanted out of life. He wanted to build a normal life with Cookie when he got out. With the money he'd bring in from this business, he could easily start rebuilding his DJ reputation. Once he was on his feet, he planned to buy a house of his own and hoped to someday live there with Cookie. He imagined possibly having a regular family life like his parents had. They would get established, buy the things they wanted, and maybe have a kid or two. He would earn a legitimate living for his family and be a great success doing what he was passionate about. He had it all figured out, finally.

Chapter 8
Love Got Me

When Nectorio got out of jail this time, he had one thing on his mind; he had to see his girl. He had done what he was supposed to for Jerome and deserved a break. He went directly to Cookie's house to find her, and though she was happy to see him, she had been sick and looked exhausted.

He felt bad for her and hoped that she hadn't been losing sleep worrying about him. He stayed with her all of that day and took care of her. They lay together on the couch cuddling and watching funny movies, which he hoped would cheer her up. He made her lunch and dinner and did whatever he could to help her feel better. It felt good being with her again, and he knew that day that being with her was where he wanted to be for a long time to come.

Nectorio spent almost all of his time with Cookie. He still worked a little with Jerome on side deals, and was working to get some jobs DJing, but she was his main focus. She always had a way of putting a smile on his face and making him feel good about himself, and that was something he loved about her.

Things were going great between them now that he was out. She had forgiven him for not telling her about his plan. Though she didn't want to know the details of what had happened in jail the second time, she listened carefully to all of his stories. He could tell that she loved and admired him, even if she didn't agree with everything he had done. They spent every day together, just like they had before he went back. Spending time with her only confirmed what he had known all along. He was totally in love with Cookie.

After about two weeks had gone by, he picked her up for dinner. He had planned to take her to a great restaurant so they could make plans for the future and just relax alone together. Cookie acted strangely quiet all the way to the restaurant, and he wondered if she was mad at him about something. He knew something was up when he ordered a bottle of expensive wine and Cookie refused to try it. He reached over and grabbed her hand and asked what was going on.

That was when Cookie told him that she was pregnant. She started sobbing then and looked around, embarrassed to be crying in public. Nectorio assured her everything would be okay, and they paid the bill without eating and left. Cookie seemed surprised to find that Nectorio was actually excited about the news. She had been afraid that he might be angry with her. She also told him that she was afraid of all of the changes this meant for them, and that she didn't know if she was truly ready to be a parent.

Nectorio was as happy as he could ever be. He realized it was time to start changing his life around, so he would have the ability to be the best father he could when the baby was born. He knew he was good in sales, so he decided to try his hand at the car business. His brother-in-law got him a job at a dealership where he was the manager.

Nectorio excelled at selling Toyotas. It was easy to figure out that selling cars was similar to selling drugs. He had the product the customers needed, and all he had to do was explain why they should get that product from him. That was where he shined. He figured he was a natural salesman. His brother-in-law was impressed with him too. Once again his family had something to be proud of him for and that felt good.

He spent his days at work perfecting his sales skills and thinking about the baby girl or boy that would be entering his life during the coming year. He tried to imagine what he or she would look like and smiled to himself, knowing that a child created by him and Cookie would have to be beautiful. He even started secretly buying little gifts for the baby. A tiny pair of Nikes here or a cool little T-shirt there. He was growing more and more excited about becoming a father.

He imagined a lucrative business and a normal life for him and the people he loved. He envisioned taking walks to the park with Cookie and the baby in the stroller, then later, sharing his stories and his music with his kid. He laughed out loud when he tried to picture a little five-year-old version of himself running around a park or basketball court causing trouble. He knew he would be a great father.

Nectorio's family was ecstatic. He was working a legitimate job and excelling at it and had a girl he loved and a baby on the way. They felt that he was finally on the right track and would be okay. With all of the stress of his getting into trouble out of the way, their relationship got back to normal. They didn't know that he still did side hustles with Jerome and Eddie, but they didn't need to know that. He was only doing it for the extra money, and nobody else needed to know about it. That was between him, Jerome, and Eddie.

Although Nectorio was trying to fly straight, he still loved the night life. His nights were filled with parties, strip clubs, and women. He had to get back out there and reconnect with old friends and, of course, make new ones. This was extremely important if he was to get his name back out there.

He wasn't living with Cookie at the time, but she was pretty sick with the pregnancy and never wanted to go out at night. He still loved being with her, but all she wanted to do was lay around and sleep, and he was going stir crazy. He started going out more and more, figuring she wouldn't miss him too much since she was always sleeping anyway.

Though he left with the best intentions most nights, once he started drinking and partying, it was hard to stay in control of his actions. Sometimes he'd end up staying out later than he had planned and doing things he normally wouldn't have done with other women.

He wasn't proud of his actions and knew he had to do his best to keep them from Cookie. He didn't want anything to come between them, and he knew it would be bad for her and the baby if she got too upset. He was the master of not getting caught, though, so he figured he'd just keep being super careful and everything would be fine.

His absence from Cookie and his partying started to get to her. Her emotions were going crazy, too, and he had heard that was from changes in hormone levels during pregnancy. Every night, she thought Nectorio was cheating on her, and this would lead to some pretty intense fights. Though he denied it, sometimes he had cheated, and it killed him to have to lie to her. The combination of alcohol and the beautiful women that surrounded him while he was out sometimes made it really hard for him to remain faithful. He didn't care about those women, though, and that was what really mattered. He still loved Cookie.

He did his best to try to get her calmed down. He tried to make up for being unfaithful when he was with her by really taking care of her and trying to make her feel special. He showered her with gifts and even started showing her some of the things he had bought for the baby.

Soon, they were fighting more than they were getting along. They were definitely drifting apart, and Nectorio started staying out later and later just to get a break from her emotional breakdowns. He was starting to think it was better for her not to have him around. He didn't want her crazy emotions to harm the baby in any way.

What Cookie did next devastated Nectorio. She went behind his back and had an abortion. Without his permission, she went and got rid of the one thing that he was looking forward to and working for. He went to her house after she wouldn't answer the phone for two days to find her lying in bed pale and sobbing. She explained tearfully that she couldn't see raising a child or having a future with him when she knew he was always with other women. He couldn't even look at her then. He wiped a tear away before it had a chance to fall from his eye, and walked out of the room. He heard her yelling his name as he walked out, but he was too upset to go back.

Nectorio couldn't believe it! It was as though someone had ripped his heart out. Not only had she killed their baby, but she had done it without talking to him first. She knew how excited he was, and that he would have never agreed to her having an abortion. Of course, that was why she didn't even give him a chance to have any input. Obviously, she didn't really love him. If she had, she would have never done it. He had to get away from her for a while, so he wouldn't do or say anything he'd regret later. He knew he needed some time to clear his head and figure out what to do next.

In spite of his shock and anger, Nectorio realized he still loved Cookie. He figured out that it was partially his fault for leaving her alone so much and for being unfaithful. He didn't agree with what she had done, but somehow, he was starting to forgive her. He decided he needed to do what he could to try to make things better between them.

Since she continuously ignored his calls, Nectorio decided it was time to go and talk to her in person. He showed up at her house with a dozen roses and a diamond bracelet for her. She gave him a hug, and he was thankful she let him in. Nectorio was so happy to see her that he wanted to do nothing but hug and kiss her. He started to kiss her passionately, and she pushed him away. She had tears in her eyes again, but Nectorio never could have predicted what came next.

Cookie broke up with him. She said she loved him, but was tired of his lying and cheating, and wanted a man she could trust. She felt like she could never have raised the baby with him, and that he wasn't capable of changing. He promised her he would change, but it was too late. She said he had violated her trust one too many times.

Anger was his response, as he screamed that her getting an abortion was the biggest violation of trust possible. The lost baby was a source of bitterness and anger between them, and no amount of fighting or begging was going to solve the problem, so he left with the bracelet he had bought for her still in his pocket.

Nectorio was heartbroken, but he vowed to show her that he was getting his life together and to get her back. He excelled at selling cars, and started putting his name out there as a DJ again with his customers and co-workers. He put on a good act for everyone during the day, but at night he felt empty and alone. He really missed Cookie and the dream of the life he had wanted to have with her.

He called Cookie every day and sometimes in the middle of the night just to show her that he was home and not out screwing around with other women. She talked to him when she was home, and led him to believe that maybe they were getting closer and closer to possibly getting back together. Eventually he noticed, though, that she was home less and less as the weeks and months wore on.

Several months had gone by when Nectorio heard from an acquaintance that Cookie had found herself a new man. Nectorio couldn't believe it. He had basically been working and living to get her back, and she had apparently never had any intention of coming back to him. The old feelings of anger and bitterness that he thought he'd gotten rid of came rushing back.

Nectorio tried to shift his focus to selling cars, working out, doing side deals with the boys, and getting back into DJing. He was doing well at all of them and could tell that people were starting to recognize his name again. The only thing missing was his girl. Though they weren't together, he kept tabs on where she was and what she was doing. He knew she would figure out soon enough that he was the right man for her. When he was out working in the clubs, women threw themselves at him. He was a hot new DJ, and everybody wanted to be with him. Although he had many opportunities, he wasn't with any other women. He wanted Cookie back.

One day, a mutual acquaintance told Nectorio something that changed his outlook on life and toward Cookie. She was pregnant again, and having her new man's baby. Nectorio went crazy, and his love for her turned to some crazy form of hate. How could she just go from him to another man and be pregnant again already? She had said all along that she wasn't ready to be a mother, but now he knew that she just wasn't ready to have a baby with him.

He had to bribe a friend of a friend to get their address, and he couldn't even see straight as he drove to their house. He had no real plan for what he would do when he got there; he just knew he had to cause her pain like she had caused him for all of these months. Nectorio wasn't a violent person, but he wasn't sure he'd be able to control himself when he saw her this time. What she had done to him was unimaginable.

He busted through the door, pushed a shocked Cookie out of the way, and attacked her boyfriend. He didn't even feel like himself as he threw punch after punch at the guy with a pregnant Cookie screaming for him to stop in the background. He didn't stop fighting until the cops pulled him off and hauled him away in cuffs while Cookie cried and watched from the doorstep. Nectorio wondered if this was how King felt so many years before and why he did the things he did.

He went to jail for a weekend, and this time he spent his time there doing nothing but sleeping and thinking. He obsessed over trying to figure out how Cookie could have another man's baby when she had killed his. He wondered if what he had felt for her was even real, and if her feelings for him had ever been real. Sure, he could've been a little more devoted, but she had to have known how much he loved her.

He decided he didn't really care what happened anymore. He didn't even care if or when he got out. He convinced himself that he would never love again, and that there really was no such thing as love. He decided that women were only good for one thing, and that was what he was going to use them for.

After that weekend in jail, his life changed drastically. His focus switched from Cookie to finding better-looking women that would be more fun. He started to sleep with every nice-looking woman he saw. He would spend a little time wining and dining them if necessary—whatever it took to get them into the bedroom. If one of them didn't like him for who he was, he made her like him. He took the time to show her what he had and what he could buy her if he got what he wanted. Once she started to seem to like him too much, he'd ditch her and find a better one. He wasn't looking for a relationship.

As Nectorio became a big-time player he started to lose sight of who he was. He figured this was the best way to forget about Cookie. Soon, one woman at a time became boring. It wasn't uncommon for Nectorio to have sex with two women and then kick them out. He'd rest for a while then and have a few drinks and a smoke, and then invite a different woman over a few hours later.

No matter how many times he did this, he didn't feel any better, which surprised him. He thought the power he had to use and hurt them would make him feel less used and hurt, but it didn't work that way. He was still haunted by memories of Cookie, who was off raising a child with some other man. He wondered what that man had that made him a capable father in Cookie's eyes, and the anger and bitterness swelled up inside of him again.

Though his job selling cars was going very well, he was getting sick of that too. He didn't feel like following all of the stupid rules and having to follow a dress code. He could make more money and wear whatever the hell he wanted working with Jerome. So he quit his job.

He didn't care what his family or friends thought about him anymore. Actually, he didn't care about anything. He had decided it was time to look out only for himself. He would focus on having fun and making as much money as he possibly could as fast as possible. He didn't need to worry about taking care of anybody else. That always seemed to backfire on him anyway. He knew what he was good at, and he would make his money and have fun along the way. This was a huge and dangerous transition in his life, but Nectorio didn't see it that way.

Chapter 9
My Music Killed My Boss

During this crazy transition in his life, Nectorio realized he had to focus totally on himself and what he wanted out of life. He knew it was time to get into the real music business. This had always been his dream, and now was his chance to actually live it out. He wasn't going to let anyone get in his way. He would continue to have fun along the way, but he wouldn't let a woman get close to him again. He knew what he had to do.

The only problem was that he was tired of small jobs. He was ready to make it big and was getting impatient. As with any other business, to make it big in the music business, a large amount of money is required. Nectorio had quit his job selling cars. He was still working with Jerome, but not making the kind of money that he needed. He saw the lifestyle Jerome was living and wanted to have it for himself.

Over time, Jerome and Nectorio became very close. Nectorio started spending almost all of his time either working with or hanging out with Jerome. Nectorio realized that he and Jerome had more in common than he had once thought. Jerome was tough and a ladies' man too. He only trusted a few people, and he was very good at running his business. Nectorio also knew that Jerome was a loyal friend. If he was on your side, he'd do anything for you. That was a quality that Nectorio respected and admired about Jerome.

Jerome knew how badly Nectorio wanted to succeed in the music business, and he also knew that he had the drive and talent to do it. They had spent many long late nights drinking, smoking, and talking about life. Jerome wanted to help Nectorio fulfill his dream. To Nectorio's surprise, he agreed to finance Nectorio.

Jerome immediately started to give Nectorio large amounts of cash to use to establish his business. This drastically changed things for Nectorio. He didn't have to wait for the things he needed to promote his name and his music anymore. Jerome was there to pay for anything Nectorio needed. With the extra money, it started getting easier and easier to get his name out there again. Soon he was booking shows not only all over the city, but in neighboring cities as well. The better business got, the more money he needed. He still wasn't making enough to finance and grow his business the way he wanted to.

Jerome continued to help him. Nectorio started to get jobs in other states and competing with other big names. If he had to fly somewhere for a show, he didn't need to worry about the plane tickets or hotel; Jerome covered it, and Nectorio didn't even have to ask. If he needed CDs pressed, Jerome paid for it. If he needed to rent a tour bus on the weekends, it was no problem. Everything was covered. Jerome made sure that they traveled in style and had everything they could possibly want or need.

Nectorio appreciated Jerome's help and got very used to having the financial help. It was easier to focus on his craft when he didn't need to worry about the financing of it, and he and Jerome were really excited about how things were going. He vowed to make sure he paid Jerome back someday when he made it big, so that he would be able to retire early and in style like Nectorio planned to do.

Throughout the process, Jerome became not only Nectorio's best friend, but also his manager for his music career. Having a manager took some of the pressure off of Nectorio so he could really focus on the music. Plus Jerome and Nectorio were completely on the same page when it came to how they wanted to promote and run the business. Nectorio knew that Jerome was one person he could totally trust who would never let him down. Jerome was like Richard had been when they were kids. It felt good to have a true best friend again.

Nectorio and Jerome were both still involved in the drug business, which was where most of the money was coming from. It wasn't long before trying to make it big in the music industry became the main focus for both of them. It became harder and harder for them to juggle both jobs, but they needed the drug money to promote their music business. They needed to be able to continue doing both until they made it big.

Business continued to pick up, but they had fierce competition. They found that they just were not making enough money to do the things they needed to do. They were trying to fund the music business through the drug trade and starting to spread themselves too thin. They both had the same goal and wanted it bad, but the stress was building.

Though his music business was starting to take off, Nectorio really wasn't making any big money from it yet. Funding the travel that was necessary with the drug money worked well enough until the travel began to affect the drug trade. When Nectorio and Jerome had to leave town to promote the music, there was always a negative impact on the traffic of the drug sales. Neither of them had anyone else they trusted one hundred percent. It was pretty clear that they couldn't continue to do both.

Jerome and Nectorio decided something needed to change if Nectorio was going to be as successful as they both knew he could be. They discussed their options and people who might be able to help them. Nectorio had lots of connections and acquaintances, but nobody he really trusted. He'd been burned one time too many and trust didn't come easy for him.

DJ Necterr

Jerome called on one of his partners for help. His was a name that was so furious it can't be mentioned. This man was a part of the biggest drug cartel in the world. Jerome must have trusted him because he set up a meeting with this guy and his associates. He asked them to advance money for Nectorio's music. He explained that Nectorio had the talent to make it really big, and it wouldn't take long for them to pay the money back. Jerome explained that the money was to promote and market Nectorio's music everywhere.

Jerome was very convincing, and it was clear that he truly believed in Nectorio and his music. This drug lord gave him a bag filled with half a million dollars. Nectorio was shocked! That was a lot of money, and now his opportunities seemed limitless. Though he was extremely excited, he was also a little worried. He knew these guys were associates of Jerome, but he also knew they were extremely dangerous. He was now under a lot of pressure to succeed as quickly as possible.

Jerome and Nectorio used a lot of the money to promote his music. They did a lot of traveling together to build up his name in the music industry. They printed CDs and started giving them away at night clubs across the country. Jerome bought an RV, and they turned it into their tour bus. It had everything imaginable in it, including two full bedroom suites. Jerome was a major ladies' man and always had to have a new woman in his presence. Strip clubs were frequent stops for Nectorio and Jerome, and they were not ashamed to pay for their women. They had some great times traveling together; times that Nectorio would never forget.

The quality of the shows, after-parties, and travel accommodations were all topnotch. Nectorio didn't keep track of what they spent since Jerome was his manager, but he was pretty sure they didn't use all of the money. Even to this day, he doesn't know what Jerome did with the rest of it. They were best friends, but even Jerome had his secrets, and he had done so much for Nectorio that he wasn't about to question him about the money. He trusted Jerome's judgment and just focused on holding up his end of the bargain. He needed to grow his business as quickly as possible, get Jerome's associates paid back, and start cashing in on his career.

The plan was for Nectorio to become a successful artist in music and eventually get a deal with a major label. Then the label would give them a lot more money than they had invested, and they would be able to pay back everything they had borrowed.

The kingpin of this deal wasn't very patient. He didn't give them enough time to make things happen. Nectorio's career was going well, but not at the pace that they expected. They wanted to see something big happen right away so they could be sure they had made a sound investment. unfortunately, the music business doesn't work that way.

They started to put pressure on Jerome daily. They wanted their money back. Then came the threats, which Jerome downplayed to Nectorio. When they realized that Nectorio's career was not booming as they were told it would be, they decided they were done waiting. They went after Jerome since he was the one who had set up the deal with them.

They used a female to set Jerome up. Anyone who knew Jerome knew that he wouldn't turn down the chance to be with a beautiful woman. He was invited to a beautiful nice young lady's house. He had told Nectorio that they would meet up later that night; he was really excited about going to meet this girl. Nectorio was happy for him. Jerome needed to relieve some stress and have a good time. They had both been working really hard and hadn't had enough time to play lately. Plus it appeared he really liked this girl.

If Jerome had a good time with this woman, Nectorio never got to hear about it. As Jerome was leaving this deceptive young lady's house, he was hit from behind by another vehicle. He had only driven for about two miles. He was slightly buzzed and extremely shocked when he got out to see what was going on. He didn't have a chance to ask any questions as he was shot several times in his chest and stomach. By the time he was found, he was already dead.

All of this happened while Nectorio was sitting at home relaxing with a couple of girls he and Jerome had met the previous week at a club with no clue that his best friend had just been a victim of cold-blooded murder. They were all drinking, and the girls were getting pretty drunk. He figured he'd have his fun with them while Jerome was out, and then get rid of them so he and Jerome could sit around and talk and drink some more or maybe even go out.

When the call came in informing him that Jerome was dead, he couldn't believe it. He wasn't himself when he kicked the shocked girls out, one of them half naked and crying. He sat in silent devastation, wondering what had happened, but deep down he knew what had happened before anyone told him.

Jerome had been stressed out lately and had dropped hints about the threats he was receiving. Nectorio knew he wasn't saying much because he didn't want him to worry, but he had sensed it had been worse than what Jerome was telling him. Jerome hadn't been himself, so they must have been harassing him pretty severely. Nectorio wished Jerome would've been honest with him about how bad it had been. Maybe then he wouldn't have let him go to this girl's house alone.

DJ Necterr

A flood of emotions overcame him. The first was rage. He picked up the kitchen chair he'd been sitting on and threw it against the wall, knocking down a framed picture of him and Jerome at a club, only making the reality of his death sink in further. Without even knowing what he was doing, he overturned the table, shattering the bottle and glasses that had been sitting on it. He got up and started pacing then, unaware that he was walking on the shattered glass until the pain of the splinters entering his feet hit him. He didn't care. He imagined it was nothing compared to what Jerome might have felt alone earlier that night outside of his car.

His phone began ringing then, and he ignored it, unwilling or maybe unable to talk to anyone at that point. Once the anger subsided and the grief set in, so did the guilt. Nectorio knew this had to have been about the money. He hadn't been able to do what he needed to do fast enough, and now Jerome was dead. His grief and anger made him irrational, and he felt completely responsible for the death of his best friend.

He had already experienced so much loss in his life, he didn't know if he could handle it this time. There was nobody he trusted enough to call. He couldn't tell his family the whole story; they didn't know or need to know what he'd been involved in. Cookie was gone. Jerome was gone. He was completely alone in his grief. He let the tears fall, but only for a short time.

Just as it always had, the anger came back to replace his sadness. When he was finished, he looked around his destroyed apartment in astonishment, too weak and tired to begin cleaning up the mess he'd made.

Then he started to sink into a dark black hole. He drank as much of the alcohol as he could find in his apartment until he passed out. When he woke up the next day, he stared at the ceiling wondering if he should get up, and if so, why. His phone kept ringing, making his pounding headache worse, and he continued to ignore it. Nobody came to check on him, which was fine; he wouldn't have answered the door anyway.

He stayed in bed for three days, getting up only to pour himself a strong drink or use the bathroom. He kept wishing there was a way to turn back time. Wishing he would've been there with Jerome to protect him. Wishing it had been him instead of Jerome, the guy who was only trying to help him achieve his goal. He drifted in and out of sleep, hoping each time he woke up that it had been a nightmare, and Jerome would be pounding on the door any minute. He wished like hell he'd hear his voice one more time, telling him to get his lazy ass out of bed so they could get to work or go out.

When enough time had passed to allow him to think straight again, Nectorio realized that

Jerome's death wasn't really his fault. These guys hadn't given them enough time. Nobody could've done what they were expecting him to do in that amount of time. He also knew that he would've reached his goal and paid them back, especially with the expertise and support of Jerome. He wouldn't let another tear fall, but he wouldn't disappoint Jerome, either. He would honor his best friend the only ways he knew how. He would reach his goal, and he would get revenge.

Nectorio wondered about the young woman they had used to lure Jerome in. Did she show him a good time first, or just have a few drinks with him and send him out into the night to be shot? He wondered if she had done it for money or maybe out of fear. Did she know what they were going to do to Jerome? How did she feel about it now? He had a hard time believing she was just as ruthless as they were, but it seemed like she had to be.

He thought about paying her a visit. Although he had never and would never really hurt a woman, he wasn't sure what he was capable of at this point. He desperately wanted to know what she could have been thinking when she agreed to play a role in the murder of his friend. He wanted everyone involved to pay; he just wasn't sure how or when. He needed time to think and a plan.

A number of associates called Nectorio shortly after the murder. He became very suspicious of the callers because they knew pretty quickly exactly what had happened. Nectorio began to wonder if they had something to do with it. He also wondered if he was next on the list. He would have to constantly watch his back; he knew that much. There was nobody he could trust.

He had known all along that these guys were not guys to mess around with, and that they probably had connections everywhere keeping tabs on him and on Jerome. Jerome's death didn't get them their money back, so he thought maybe they were just trying to send Nectorio a very strong message. He was very cautious about what he said to anyone who called and how he reacted to the details they shared about Jerome's death. He was back to trusting nobody but himself, and that was a lonely and desperate place to be, but he'd been there before and survived.

During the weeks following Jerome's death, Nectorio desperately worked to rebuild his mental and physical strength. He increased his workouts and tried to channel his pain and anger into his music. His nights were filled with nightmares. He relived the night of Jerome's death every night in his sleep. The dream always started with Jerome kissing that beautiful lady goodnight. Then he'd get into his car, turn up the radio as loud as it would go, and start singin' along. Then came the fierce lunge forward as they smashed ruthlessly into his car. He'd get out, a mixture of rage and confusion on his face, and be assaulted by gunfire. Sometimes in the dream, Nectorio would jump out of the car and get between Jerome and the gunfire. Other times he'd arrive on the scene minutes too late, only to look down at the bloody corpse of his dear friend. Those were the nights he'd wake up in a cold sweat.

Despite the dreams and his anger, Nectorio decided that he would survive again. He would become better and stronger. He would fight back. He refused to give up and let Jerome's death be in vain. He knew he had only himself to depend on now, but that was okay. If nobody else got close to him, he'd be able to focus on his goals, and there would be nobody else to lose. No matter what it took, he would continue what he and Jerome started, and he would succeed.

Chapter 10
The New Boss Is Here

After the night his best friend was killed, Nectorio was ready for war. He got back to work out on the streets. He had a new passion for his work and an extreme desire to build up the business he and Jerome had started.

Before he knew it, he was asked to work for the same people that he believed were responsible for killing Jerome. He could hardly believe it, and he knew he had to think carefully about his next move. He was very suspicious of them because he knew they were connected to the ones that had given Jerome the money. He was careful to hide his suspicions, though; he'd learned a lot from Jerome.

He decided he was going to do what he had to in order to work his way to the top, and then he'd find a way to get even for what had happened to Jerome. Besides, the best way to keep track of them and what they were doing would be to work with them for a while. That way, he could—he hoped—be sure he wasn't their next target.

Nectorio knew the reason they wanted him to work for them was because he was a good hustler, and he could get rid of drugs real fast. This was a skill that got him through the hard times when nothing else could. When they gave him the drugs, he sold them faster than most of their other drug dealers. He had the right connections and the drive to get the job done quickly and efficiently. He was just biding his time working for them; he had no plans to do it for a long time.

After a short while, they asked him to take over the "boss" position. Nectorio refused and started an all-out war with them. In his mind, he knew he was overpowered by them. They had a much bigger crew than he did. He also knew they had more guns and other weapons and much more money. Nectorio didn't care, though. He was so angry that he thought he could take them down, and this became his new focus.

This was when things started to get a little strange and dangerous. Nectorio would be out with friends or his crew at a night club just minding his own business and having a good time. A fight would break out and turn into a shoot-out. Nectorio was not involved in most of the shoot-outs. The people involved were people in his crew, though, or friends of friends. He was pretty sure innocent people were killed in these shoot-outs, but not a hundred percent sure. It bothered him to know that people who had nothing to do with the business or with what had happened to Jerome might be getting hurt. He worked hard to block those feelings out, though, because there was no way he was going to give up on his mission.

Nectorio knew that the only way to take down someone so powerful was to set them up. He had his crew, but he needed to build it up in order to really take down the most powerful of them all. He started to work harder and harder to make good connections and build up a network of people he hoped he could trust. Just as Jerome had done with him, he lured them in with the promises of lots of money and an amazing lifestyle.

The situation became more dangerous for Nectorio. He was starting to put his family and many of his friends at risk. He knew that this war he was involved in had no rules. When at war in the streets, the enemy may do anything to win. They could set up family members and friends to set him up. It was impossible to know just how heartless the enemy was, especially when he had a strong feeling that innocent people were already dying.

He had to put friends and family in different houses to secure them, just in case. Even though there wasn't much happening to his family at that time, he was more worried about them than anything. He didn't want to be the one to cause them trouble, and he didn't want to lose anyone else in his life. He knew he wouldn't be able to live with himself if anything ever happened to his parents or siblings; he'd already lost a best friend in this war.

To their dismay, Nectorio couldn't tell his family what was going on. He didn't want them to know what he was involved in. They wouldn't approve, and their knowing could make things even more difficult and dangerous for them. They knew something was very wrong, though, and begged him to tell them what was going on. The fact that he couldn't drove a wedge between him and his parents again, which killed him because he knew they were hurt and worried. He just kept telling himself that it was for their own good, and someday when he made his millions, he'd set them up really well to make up for it. Right now, they'd never understand.

It only took Nectorio a couple of months to find out that war was not the answer to this situation. He had a lot of scares, threats, and family members who were starting to get very worried about him being killed or hurt badly. They were also worried about him getting into the kind of trouble that could get him put away in jail or even prison for a very long time. Although they didn't know exactly what was going on, they had strong suspicions.

During this time, Nectorio had many scares. He would be out with friends and have to watch them get arrested, hoping and praying that they wouldn't sell him out so he would be next. There were several times where shoot-outs occurred, and bullets missed either him or his friends by inches. All of this was because of the war he had started. This made him feel a little guilty and nervous that something really bad might happen to a friend or someone who worked for him. Though these were scary times, he felt a rush of adrenaline every time something happened, which just renewed his desire for revenge. Once again he was filled with a crazy mixture of emotions that he'd experienced many times before in his life.

Throughout these terrifying experiences, he knew it was a bad idea to continue what he had started. He couldn't stop, though; his anger and thirst for revenge was too strong. He was ready for anything and everything and didn't care at all about his own safety. As long as he kept those he cared about safe, everything would be fine, even if he had to take a bullet to do it.

Nectorio eventually became very paranoid due to the stress of worrying about everybody so much. He started receiving threatening phone calls on a daily basis not only targeting him, but also, just as he had feared, his loved ones.

One night, Nectorio had taken some good friends out on the town. He took them to a great restaurant for dinner. He loved treating his friends when he had extra money. They then went to an awesome party. After lots of drinking, dancing, and a dip in the pool, they were ready to head to his house for an after-party. They were laughing at some stupid joke as they stumbled to the car holding on to each other for support. As always, the girls seemed a little more tipsy than the guys.

Suddenly, bullets came flying out of nowhere. Someone was shooting at Nectorio and his friends.

Nectorio wasn't sure if it was because they were in the wrong neighborhood or because of his beefs with other crews, but he was pretty sure it had something to do with him. No one was injured, but they were all pretty shaken up, especially the ladies. These friends that he was with were very innocent and had nothing to do with his problems. Nectorio felt terrible. His friends were terrified and had no idea they were in danger just by being with him. They didn't deserve it. He knew he'd have to be more careful about where he went out from then on, as well as who he took with him. This was just one more sacrifice he'd have to make in his life to be successful and protect those he cared about.

Nectorio decided that to fight fire with fire, he needed to get even further into the business. He gathered up his army. It didn't take him long to get a new team once he utilized all of his connections, both new and old. He then built his name back up in the streets as the go-to guy for any drug needed.

After about six months, business was better than ever. He had taken Jerome's business and grown it to new heights. He was the new boss! He knew that Jerome would be proud of him, and that made him feel a little better about what had happened. Of course, it didn't lessen the pain of losing his friend.

He was still working for the guys he believed to be responsible for Jerome's death, but now he was the boss, and they were the suppliers. He got everything from them, but still ran his own drug business. Soon they stopped harassing him. They made a truce as both sides realized it was better to just settle everything. Financially, they would all win that way. The fighting had become a lose-lose situation for everyone, and Nectorio did not want to see anyone else he cared about get hurt. Money became his new sole motivation. He was going to make as much of it as quickly as he possibly could.

Nectorio wasn't sure if they were still worried about the money Jerome had borrowed. He didn't think they saw him as the person to blame anymore, but he wasn't sure. He knew he couldn't truly trust anyone. He believed they needed him just to make money because he sold faster than everyone else, and that was a good position for him to be in.

Life had changed drastically for Nectorio once again. Suddenly, everyone knew him. No one knew how he got his money, but they knew he had money. He must have been something like a boss the way he rolled. He had armed security always with him when he went out at night. No more worrying about himself or his friends being in danger. Now he was the one to watch out for.

DJ Necterr

Nectorio was finally the new man in charge. He was the top man right under the supplier, and it had only taken him three months, which was amazing by anyone's standards. He was back to believing he could do anything he set his mind to.

He decided it was time to start enjoying life again after struggling and living in fear and anger for so long. He stayed at the best hotels whenever he felt like it. He didn't need a reason. He had his own money to play with now. He slept with the sexiest women. He never had to go looking for them either; they seemed to be all around him, wherever he went. They knew who he was, and they were all interested in going home with him. It was a little entertaining the way they competed for his attention. A few of them tried to get close to him, but he always pushed them away. There was no way he was falling into that trap ever again. He didn't need anyone but himself to be happy.

Soon Nectorio was living in a huge, beautiful house. He had indoor and outdoor pools and hot tubs and a full basketball court. The theater room was big enough to seat fifty of his friends. He hosted the biggest and best parties ever with an endless supply of drugs, booze, great music, and beautiful women.

He had arrived. No more Nectorio. He now had everyone call him Necterr. In Greek mythology, nectar was a drink given to the gods. In fact, it was one of their favorite treats. It was believed that any

DJ Necterr

mortal lucky enough to partake of it would become immortal. Nectorio felt that he was on top, so he was the closest thing to being a god. He also felt invincible.

Nectorio felt he was untouchable and started beefs with everyone. He trained his crew to have the mentality to use any means necessary. He no longer cared what happened to anyone who tried to cross him; he'd learned that nobody else really cared, so why should he? The small innocent boy who had been shocked at a wedding so long ago was gone. Nectorio was learning to be hard and emotionless. He'd made it to the top, he was living the good life, and he was going to do whatever it took to keep it that way.

If the small cats wanted to find a way to get money, Nectorio let them. It was cool that they did it under his name. When the smaller people did something wrong, they always blamed the boss. At this time, it was not a problem for Nectorio. He actually enjoyed being blamed. This gave him even more chances to prove that he was completely untouchable.

If his friends wanted to rob people, he let them. If they wanted to do anything to get money, even if it was dangerous or ruthless, he allowed it. He didn't care. If there was something or someone he didn't like, he would put it out there that he didn't like them. He would talk shit about a lot of people to the people he knew would go and tell them. He didn't care what type of trouble this would get him into. It was all like a game to him.

Nectorio's new attitude and behavior got him into a lot of beefs across the country, but he wasn't worried. He started to receive threats again, but most of the threats didn't bother him because he knew he was completely untouchable. He didn't care at all; when a threat was made, he would make one right back. He made sure his threats were carried out when necessary so that he would be taken seriously by everyone.

Wanting to stay connected to the club scene, he was DJing about three days a week as the new and improved Necterr. At times, he felt a little exhausted, but he kept pushing himself hard; he wanted it all. He eventually started doing less DJing and a lot of party hosting since he had become well known again. This didn't bother him at all. The parties were fun and great exposure for him.

His drug business still interfered a little with his progress as a DJ, but he was still in the club scene. He was not behind the tables as much as he used to be, but now on the stage hyping the crowd as a host and an MC, which he found he was really good at. The crowds loved him, and he loved doing it. The best was when they started getting drunk or high, and he could really get them going. Nectorio loved his new life, but it was on the stage where he felt most comfortable, as if he was really only himself when he was up there working with the crowds and the music. It was after those nights that he slightly questioned himself and how he was making his money. It was too late to turn back, though; he was on the top and intended to stay there.

Nectorio's relationship with his family was shaky at the time because he was all over the place and didn't have much time to spend with them. When he did spend time with them, they only became more worried because they could see a new look in his eyes. It was the look of someone who had no fear and didn't care about anything. He tried to hide it when he was around them, but it wasn't something he could hide; it was who he had become. That look worked well in the business, but it only worried his family more. Although they didn't know exactly what he was doing, they had their suspicions. They could see a huge difference in both his lifestyle and his attitude. Whenever any of them tried to talk to him about it he just lied and said his music business was thriving. His dad stopped looking him in the eye; maybe he was afraid of what he might see. It was different with his mom, though. She seemed to be able to look right through him. It killed him to see her eyes fill with tears when they said goodbye each time. It reminded him of the good old days in jail and the pain he had caused her then.

If they pushed too hard for information, he kept his distance for a while. He would call occasionally to let his mother know he was okay, but he didn't share much information about where he was or what he was doing. They didn't need to know what he was doing. He didn't want to disappoint or worry them any more than he had already.

After awhile he stopped trying to lead a double life with his family and close friends. There was no reason for him to try to be the old Nectorio for anyone; he would be Necterr everywhere and to everyone. If someone didn't like it, he didn't care. They'd have to learn to deal with it or stay away from him. He had finally convinced himself that to stay on top, he had to be cold and emotionless.

No more being afraid, sad, or lonely. The past was the past. He would protect himself, his family, and those who were loyal to him. He would also protect his position at the top. He'd worked hard for it and gotten used to the lifestyle. He would do anything to stay right where he was.

Sometimes in the early morning hours he'd lay awake and smile up at the ceiling, amazed at what he had accomplished and who he had become. Then an uneasy empty feeling would set in and try to steal his happiness. It was then that he'd pop a couple of sleeping pills, or pain pills, and drift off, hoping to gain some much needed rest. After all, he had to get up and do it all again the next day. He was the boss.

Chapter 11
Business Goes Bad

Eight months into business, Necterr got some disturbing news. The murderers of his best friend were arrested. The word on the street, which always traveled fast, was that they were arrested on an unrelated drug case. When each of them was pressured separately, someone had turned into an informant.

At first, Necterr was elated. Maybe justice had finally been served, and Jerome could rest in peace. He threw a huge party in honor of his fallen friend and the arrest of his murderers. It was one of the best parties he'd ever had, and when he passed out that night after plenty of booze, dancing, and sex, it was with a smile on his face. He knew he was in the comfort of his beautiful home while those guys were tossing and turning on jail cots where they would hopefully stay for a very long time.

The next day, though, in the haze of a nasty hangover, Necterr became uneasy. He knew what kind of people these guys and their associates were. They wouldn't go down without a fight. He also knew that because of the business, he could be seen as directly connected to them. What if the cops really started investigating them and their activities?

It would be easy to follow the trail directly to him, the top dealer. He didn't want any trouble now. He was just starting to really get used to the good life.

He knew these guys weren't the type to protect him or his name either. They definitely wouldn't be happy about his recent success. In this competitive business, almost everyone was the jealous type. He was sure they knew how well he was doing; he hadn't tried to hide it at all. He began to slightly regret some of his recent behavior, fearing that he may have really pissed off the wrong people and desperately hoping he was overreacting.

He hadn't overreacted at all. Things ended up being even worse than Necterr had imagined. When Jerome's killers went to jail, they made up an elaborate story in an attempt to get themselves out. The gist of their story was that Necterr had hired them to kill Jerome. They claimed that he had felt Jerome was in his way because he wanted to be on top, not second in the chain of command. They desperately wanted out of jail, but there was something they and their associates wanted even more. They wanted Necterr put away for good. He had become too cocky and fierce competition in the business. They felt he needed to be put in his place so they could prosper.

Of course, this story was totally false; however, to the police and FBI investigators, the story was good enough. Necterr was part of a criminal empire, and they had looked very carefully into his activities. They knew all about his "criminal" background. They had already suspected that Jerome's murder was a murder for hire. Now they had the two guys who were hired in custody, pointing the finger at him. All of this added up to a no-win situation for him. They didn't need any more proof than what they had to arrest him. That's exactly what they did, and the worst part was, they seemed to enjoy it.

In September of 2005, Necterr was sitting at his house with a small group of friends when the doorbell rang. He figured someone else had heard he was hosting a party and strolled to the door to let them in. Uniformed officers stood at the door rather than friends, and Necterr felt a lump harden in his throat. He was arrested on the spot for conspiracy and the murder of his best friend while his new friends watched in horror, shocked and helpless.

Necterr was stuck in a jail cell with a million dollar bail, and there wasn't much he could do about it at the time. What upset him even more than the arrest itself was the fact that anyone could possibly accuse him of harming, let alone killing, his dear friend Jerome. He knew how ridiculous the charges were, but he also knew that his activities wouldn't make him look good in the eyes of the law.

He answered every question honestly, but it didn't matter. It reminded him of back when he was in school. He didn't have a chance to prove himself.

Just like most of the teachers had back then, the authorities had already made up their minds about him. He was in deep this time. Necterr knew he hadn't done everything right, but it seemed like no matter what, he somehow always ended up in an impossible situation.

In jail, or at least in the county jail that he was in, Asians got along with the blacks. Since Necterr knew this, he wasn't surprised when a guy named Kao quickly tried to befriend him. He thought Kao was okay, but Necterr was smart enough not to trust anyone too much.

Kao started to be wherever Necterr was, and he was always watching him. This was very unnerving, and Necterr started to get suspicious, but he told himself maybe he was just lonely or a little weird. Necterr definitely wasn't looking to make friends, but he tried to be nice to the guy. He had bigger things to worry about than some weird guy following him around; he was in jail for murder.

While Necterr was sitting in jail in his dorm room full of about thirty guys, he was involved in a fight. Suspiciously, the fight appeared to be for no reason at all. He was merely making his bed when an inmate suddenly got into Necterr's personal space in the area around his bed and started trouble by pushing him so hard from behind that he flew over the bed—falling on top of him. The crowd erupted with cheers as if they were at a pro football game as he started pounding the guy in the face, head, and chest. His rage had taken over, and he didn't know if he'd be able to stop until this guy was dead. His vision was blurred, and he felt as if he suddenly had water in his ears as the cheers became muffled with his increasing anger. Somehow, his enemy broke free of his punches and swiftly threw him back against the wall again, and the roles were reversed. It was then that Necterr saw his face. The already swollen and bruised eyes of Kao looked back at him with sheer hate. His bottom lip was split open and blood poured down his shirt, but he was coming back at Necterr for more.

Confused, Necterr quickly scanned his memory for anything that he might have said or done to push Kao over the edge. There was nothing. He took a hard hit to the stomach, then let loose on Kao again. He pushed him to the ground and began slamming his head into the cement floor while yelling, "Why?" into his face. The crowd continued to roar and clap, enjoying the violence much more than Necterr was.

Kao smiled and reached for something in his pocket. When Necterr saw the shiny object in Kao's bloodied hand, he sat back, exhausted, waiting for him to attack. Maybe this was it. Maybe his story would end here, with thirty onlookers cheering while he took his last breath. Maybe his mother and father would read about his gruesome and senseless death in the paper in a day or two. He pictured his successful siblings at his funeral, sadly wondering what had gone wrong with him.

Necterr didn't want that to happen, but he was tired. He was tired of working so hard only to be knocked down just when things started happening for him. He was tired of disappointing his family. He was tired of losing people he cared about. Most of all, he was tired of not being able to truly trust anyone—always having to second guess people was exhausting for him. He wondered for a minute if death would be the easiest route at that point, and then he snapped out of it and got ready to continue the fight.

Kao seemed to be having second thoughts of his own. Breathing heavily, he glanced at the shiny object in his hand and then crawled backwards and leaned against the wall. He sat like that, staring at Necterr until the guards came to haul them both away for questioning.

Necterr figured he was lucky this guy didn't have enough heart to go through with a murder in jail and risk his life. If he had, there had been enough time for him to do it while Necterr had sat in a daze imagining his funeral.

Word in jail travels even faster than word on the streets. Necterr was told that this guy was supposed to have beaten him to death or stabbed him. Either way would have done the job, but it didn't happen. Even though he was already in jail, the people really responsible for Jerome's murder were not going to risk anything. They had quickly put money on Necterr's head to have him killed while he was there so they wouldn't have to deal with him if and when he got out.

So, he had his answer. Kao wasn't just some weird and lonely inmate. He was hoping to make a ton of money by killing Necterr. He wondered what kind of life he had before coming to jail. What would have made him desperate enough to kill for money? For a moment, he almost felt sorry for the guy.

Kao had spoken to Necterr about a wife and two young children one recent day as Necterr half listened, trying to fake interest. Kao was supposedly in jail because of a robbery that had gone wrong. He had been armed, but claimed he had no intention of using his weapon for anything but scaring the sales clerk at a convenience store. In the end, he had panicked and shot the guy three times, not killing him, but sending him into a coma.

He had a sad look in his eyes as he had talked about being caught in a system where he couldn't get ahead and support his family. Had these all been lies, or was that what he wanted this blood money for? Necterr decided it didn't matter. At least he didn't have to be nice to the guy anymore. Maybe he wouldn't even see him again since he'd been moved to a separate dorm.

Necterr lay in bed that night trying to clear his mind. He couldn't believe this was happening to him again. Just when everything had started going so smoothly for him, his life had taken another one hundred eighty degree turn for the worse. Not only was he in jail again, but there were people who desperately wanted him dead.

Just because Kao hadn't been successful didn't mean there weren't others on the inside waiting to take his place and do the job. In fact, Necterr knew there were probably several just waiting for the chance. He had to live on the defense, watching every move that was made. He felt a little paranoid. Now if someone even looked at him a second too long, that person became a suspect in Necterr's mind.

Necterr was worried about what he could do if and when he got out. His businesses, both as a dealer and a DJ, would suffer. He would have to be extremely careful once he was out, which would make it hard to pick up where he had left off. Plus, he'd obviously need to find new suppliers, which wasn't always easy to do. It would be especially hard to do in secret.

He also worried about his family. It would kill his mother to know that his life might be in danger. He knew these were the type of people who might threaten or hurt his family and friends as well, just to get to him. He knew he'd rather be dead himself than have anyone else close to him get hurt or killed. He had to figure out a way to beat these people at their own game. It would be hard now that they had been caught and had tried to frame him, though. He knew the police and FBI would be watching him extremely closely.

Necterr considered his options carefully. The swirling mass of emotions had come back to haunt him again. It was hard for him to think straight and even harder to control his anger. He knew that there was nothing he could have done to prevent this from happening, short of being in Jerome's place the night he was killed. He hadn't been prepared to have to fight to keep his position as boss, though. He had worked so hard to get there, and now it was all in jeopardy again.

Nectorio knew these guys wouldn't stop until they got what they wanted. There didn't seem to be any clear answers. He felt helpless and hopeless, but continued to wear his tough-guy mask. He couldn't afford to let anyone around him see his vulnerability.

As soon as Necterr heard of the hit out on his head and he could make a call, he immediately called one of his people to get him bailed out. His bail was set at one million dollars. He paid his ten percent bail bonds fee and got out.

Since the people he did business with had a hit out on his head, he could not conduct business as usual. These people had been his suppliers. It was as if someone had hit a rewind button on his life, and he would have to start all over once again if and when he got out of this mess.

At this time, business was really bad. He could not "re-up," and he had very little product left. He had to learn to work with what he had. Luckily, he had always worked with a lot of weight, so it lasted for a few weeks. The money was slow, but he still had a little. He'd have to try hard to make it last while using what he could to keep his business alive.

Necterr spent his days stressing all day long and doing a lot of thinking about what his next move would be. He had people he thought he could trust, but he just wasn't one hundred percent sure. He had to find another supplier. He needed to do this quickly and carefully because there was a hit on his head.

Along with those problems, he couldn't show his face in many places because he had money out to kill him. This impacted his music business as well. He could only DJ or MC maybe once every other week. He had to stay completely low key. In his heart and mind he knew that there were plenty of other talented people out there just waiting for the chance to take his place. Now while they were working their way up doing what he had loved the most, he had to hide like a common criminal. It made him sick.

Necterr had a little money saved up and a very small amount of drugs left. He started selling out of his own hand and even out of his own car sometimes just like he had in the beginning.

Necterr's family didn't know what was going on. They just saw that something was very wrong. His lifestyle had drastically changed again. They figured he was struggling with life at this time, which was true. It was a really rough time. They just didn't realize how bad things really were.

Necterr had to go into hiding. He moved from one female's house to another. The females' houses seemed to be safer, and he'd hopefully have less of a chance of being found. Though they were all very kind and generous to him, he didn't get too friendly with any of them. He remembered all too well what had happened to Jerome, and he was never really sure if he was walking into a safe situation or being deceived like his friend had been.

He didn't go to many places; it was just too risky. Necterr secluded himself as much as possible. Though he would have liked to visit his parents and let them know he was okay, he didn't. He couldn't take the chance of being followed there and putting them in danger.

It was a horrible way to live, and Necterr started to feel depressed. It was especially difficult because he had been living the good life just a few weeks before with seemingly no end in sight. Now that life was out of reach again, and he spent all of his time either worrying about being killed or being bored out of his mind in hiding while the outside world went on without him.

He tried to block out memories of all the fun he'd been having and the people who had seemed to admire him so much. Where were they all now? He didn't notice any of them rushing to his side to help him. Were they all just cowards or users? Maybe they were just smart, he decided. He couldn't blame them for wanting to keep themselves and their families out of harm's way. In a matter of days his reputation and career had taken a huge hit. He didn't know how he would do it, but he had to find a way to save them both.

Chapter 12
The Music Business

After a thorough investigation of unproven events and false accusations from the other suspects, the charges against Necterr were dropped. He breathed a deep sigh of relief when he realized he would not even have to go to court. His accusers ended up staying in jail due to a number of other unrelated yet serious charges against them. Their plan to frame Necterr and get an early release for being witnesses to the murder had failed. Their major flaw was that they did not have their stories straight, and they didn't match up at all when told in isolation.

To Necterr's knowledge, Jerome's murder remains unresolved to this day. Though he didn't want to, Necterr had to distance himself from those people and the case because doing otherwise only got him into trouble. Not to mention that he still had never found his childhood friend, Richard.

Necterr continued to lie really low for over six months. It was hard to do, since he was so used to being in the center of the action before he was framed. He tried to wait patiently and worked on clearing his name from the streets. He stayed clean and made sure that nobody could connect the dots and find him.

As hard as it was to lie low, he knew this was something he had to do because the money on his head was due to the fact that he was a major liability. When he was arrested for a murder that he had nothing to do with, he had become one, since he knew who actually did it. In their eyes, if he talked to the police and the police decided to listen, he could ruin their entire drug empire. He knew that nobody could actually prove they were linked to Jerome's murder even though he absolutely knew this was true. He also knew that no matter what, he would not turn into a snitch, not even for his best friend.

Necterr really didn't care about ruining them anyway. All he wanted to do was clear his name and get on with his life and career. Those were the things that Jerome would've wanted for him. As far as he was concerned, time was precious, and he had wasted a bunch of it in jail and hiding out. He knew he was getting older, not younger, and the competition was fierce out there. He was more than ready to get back to work. This time he planned to be more careful and avoid getting mixed up with anyone who would bring him down again.

Once his name was completely cleared, Necterr was finally able to show his face again with no more money on his head. All his beef at that time was squashed. He decided to get back into business, but he knew he needed to be careful. He figured he needed to try a different approach so his recent enemies wouldn't see him as competition and try to come after him again. He had given it a lot of thought while in hiding, since he had so much time on his hands to think, and he believed he had some great ideas.

He got out of the weed business right away and instead went into the pill business. Necterr had frequently bought Ecstasy for his own personal use. He knew how popular it was and figured it would be pretty easy to sell. He decided this was the key to his new business.

He noticed right away how much easier the pills were to transport. He also knew they'd be easier to sell than most other types of drugs because of the convenience factor. Ecstasy didn't need to be injected, smoked, or snorted. All his customers needed to do was swallow it and wait for it to take effect. They could do this anywhere. It couldn't be easier to sell.

He knew all of the mid-level pill dealers from buying from them in the past. He also knew that if he could get a good deal with a major supplier, he would be right back into the game with a new and fairly risk-free business. Necterr used the few connections he could trust to get hooked up with suppliers, but he did all of the work himself. Before he knew it, he was selling over 150,000 pills a month.

Necterr found out that an industry that used a lot of his business was the music business, which was convenient, since that was where he ultimately wanted to be spending his time and using his talents. It made sense that Ecstasy would be in high demand for artists and their fans. This "feel good drug" made everyone incredibly happy and was known to help people relate to each other better. Logically, this could reduce the number of disputes that broke out nightly at concerts and clubs. Necterr saw this as something that music did also, so combining the effects of the drug with music was a win-win experience for most people. This is why they always came back for more, which made it a win-win situation for Necterr as well.

For the artists, it boosted their self-esteem, and relaxed them so that if they had an anxiety attack, it would disappear within minutes. Best of all, the club scene couldn't be better, with users able to dance all night long without worrying about or wanting sleep or food. With Ecstasy, they had an endless supply of energy.

Necterr started making many connections through networking on the computer. He often found himself in the right place at the right time. He soon befriended a lady by the name of Deborah James. She co-owned and ran a clothing store in Harlem, New York, with her son, Juelz. Necterr would visit the store frequently and talk to her about things she could do to boost her son's career. He knew Juelz Santana was a rapper with a lot of talent and a huge career ahead of him.

Necterr became a friend and business associate to Juelz. He started making frequent calls to his brother, whom they called Twin, and stayed in touch with his mom. He began getting Juelz a lot of shows. The more shows he got for him, the more money they made, so they were happy to maintain a friendly relationship with Necterr. This relationship was somewhat beneficial to Necterr as well. It helped get him out into the right places where he could do a lot of networking.

Soon after Necterr developed a relationship with Deborah and Juelz, he became very close to a lot of the members of the Dip Set family. They saw how he was helping Juelz get shows and saw him in the right places at the right times. Juelz rarely did shows alone, and Necterr was always at his concerts. Juelz always had his friends around him, and this included his group members. It didn't take long for all of them to get to know Necterr and recognize his amazing people skills and talents.

Necterr had learned to quickly build good relationships and network. He would just call and help set shows up for the Dip Sets or do whatever they needed him to do. He was efficient and effective, and everyone seemed to notice that when they started working with him. They were small things, but he knew that every little thing got him that much closer to the scene that he desperately wanted to become a major part of. He knew how to be patient and start small in order to work his way up. He'd done it countless times before.

Necterr was at all of Dip Set's shows, concerts, and after parties. This kept him very busy on the weekends, which was fine with him. He had enough free time Monday through Wednesday and even during the daytime on the weekends. This was helping him build his reputation back up in a hurry. For several months, he was kept around as their after party DJ and one of their new west coast artists. He was on his own natural high as his business and career started to take off again.

During the time that he spent around them at their after-parties and shows, he supplied around a total of 10,000 pills. He had a good supplier and would sell all different types. Every shipment he got in included several different types, which was great. He again became the go-to guy who was known for keeping everyone happy by giving them exactly what they wanted. Necterr was starting to relax and have fun again. The shows were packed. The clubs were always filled with tons of sexy women and a lot of weed. There were plenty of pills for whoever wanted or needed them, and he loved being an important part of the scene again.

The after-parties were even crazier because they would always get more love at the after- party at the club than at the concert or show. While the concerts might have three thousand to fifteen thousand fans with three- to five-foot stages, the after-parties were much smaller with a maximum of a thousand people at the bigger clubs. The atmosphere was much more intimate.

At the clubs, most fans could get right next to the artists in the VIP areas. All it would take for a sexy woman or several of them was to ask, and they could be right there with the artists and Necterr in VIP. Males always wanted to hang around them too. All the guys would have to do is buy a few bottles at the club, and they could be in the VIP area right next to them also.

It was all good as long as the artists did their thing on stage. While they kept the crowd going, Necterr spent his time mingling with half of the club and getting rid of as many pills as he could. His job seemed to get easier and easier as the nights went on. He met some fun and amazing people and didn't mind being constantly surrounded by beautiful women.

Necterr loved his life again. After the after-parties at the club, there were always the after-parties at the hotels. There were always plenty of sexy women anxious to get close to them at least for the night. Some of them wanted more than just one night with Necterr, but he had promised himself long ago that he wouldn't get into another relationship. He didn't have time for that. He was just happy that once again his nights were filled with lots of music, sex, and drugs. This was like that rock star life that he had only seen glimpses of in the past.

Being at a lot of shows, concerts, and parties, Necterr starting meeting celebrities. There were always celebs that would pop up at these events. One of the first celebrities he met was Lloyd Banks. Lloyd Banks was very disrespectful to women, and at that time in his life, Necterr was too. It was nothing for him to call a woman a bitch for no reason to her face, just as Lloyd did. Once, when Necterr was at a hotel in Los Angeles with Lloyd Banks and a few of the homies, they had him call up some women. Two models and three of four of their friends came to the hotel room. The girls acted snobby at first, and the first thing Lloyd said after catching wind of their attitudes was, "What's wrong with these funny ass bitches?" Necterr's perception was that Lloyd was upset that these women weren't immediately all over him.

Some other celebrities he worked with were 50 Cent, Memphis Bleek, and Lil Wayne. Necterr never really saw any of them as celebrities, though. He didn't view them as any more special or important than regular people. He just saw them as regular people with a little more money and millions of followers.

One of these people was Lil Wayne. Lil Wayne was a frequent pill popper and coke user. He was actually Necterr's first regular rap customer. He would buy the coke, pop a pill, and wrap his coke in

DJ Necterr

a weed blunt so nobody knew he was doing coke. As far as his personality went, Lil Wayne was down to earth, but very confident and cocky. He was always ready to work and get in the studio. He seemed to be making music in his head 24/7. Like everyone else, he saw Necterr as a good connection to have.

Necterr also met a few other artists at the time. He met Chingy, Twista, so many he couldn't even keep track of them all. It was tougher trying to figure out who he hadn't met yet.

Most of the artists liked having Necterr around because he always had the women around him, or at least the drugs for the women. He was a good connection to have around and they all knew it. Some of those artists did not know what he was doing, or they knew and didn't care. He didn't care either. He was enjoying life, making plenty of cash, and in the middle of the music scene.

Only people Necterr dealt with knew about his business. His friends and family thought he was just very convincing and good at selling himself to these labels. They all thought he was traveling so much because he was really in the business. He kept telling himself that he was really in the business and the pills were just a part of it. He knew that his parents were mostly just relieved to see he was getting back on his feet and didn't appear to be in danger anymore.

After months of hard work, Necterr had

turned his drug business into a legitimate music business. Since he had become friends with a number of artists, he started his own booking business. This was easy for him to do as he had been getting to know the artists so well. Most people wouldn't know the first step to figuring out how to contact the artists, so they always had to go through booking agents. Since Necterr's name was already flowing through the entertainment business, it was a natural step for him to become a booking agent. People started contacting him to book the artists.

He then found out that even though he was friends with a lot of these artists, they would only give him good deals for favors in return. In return for lowering their average show price, he would give them an after-party full of pills. He wasn't surprised that many of their friendships came with ulterior motives, just occasionally slightly annoyed. Then he reminded himself how much money he was making, and it was all okay again.

Even though business was booming again, Necterr felt slightly lonely. He couldn't consider anyone in the industry true friends. In the drug business, his motto had to be "Don't trust nobody that you had just met." He couldn't let anything jeopardize his incredible new business. It was hard to understand why he couldn't be successful and have good friends at the same time, though.

Business then started booming—legit and

illegal. He made more money than he had ever made before. He found himself making about twenty to thirty thousand a week. He learned to spend it just as quickly as he made it. He spent thousands at strip clubs and even more gambling. Of course, he had to spend some of it for his own personal drug use as well. If his mother needed money because something needed to be fixed at home, he would give it to her, but that only happened occasionally. He was making so much money that he didn't see a need to save or invest it. It felt as though there was a never-ending supply of it. Necterr figured he would never have to worry about money again in his lifetime.

A lot of club promoters started asking Necterr how he got such deals on artists. This concerned him for a while but he became good at just telling people he was good friends with them. He could be extremely convincing when he needed to. As far as he could tell, no one ever figured it out.

Getting caught didn't really cross Necterr's mind. The way he was doing business was seamless, and he figured he had finally found a fail-proof way to succeed. He was making a ridiculous amount of money, meeting all of the greats in the business, and having the time of his life.

He was also DJing and MCing at this time, doing pretty much everything he wanted. The best part about it was that his name was getting put on major concert flyers around the world. Once again

Necterr was well on the way to living out his dream. He was pretty sure he had proven that nothing and nobody could keep him down, but that didn't keep him from continuing to watch his back.

Still, something was nagging at him. It would creep up on him late at night or early in the morning the few times he was alone. He had come back from a major setback again and was living the life that so many people only imagined having, but something was bothering him. He was having a great time, but for some reason, Necterr knew deep down that happiness was still eluding him. He wondered if there was really something wrong with him. Who in his right mind wouldn't be happy in his shoes? He tried to ignore these feelings each time they popped up, telling himself to just relax and enjoy the ride. He knew all too well how things could change overnight for him, so he figured he needed to live it up and be grateful that his hard work was paying off. He just needed to keep focusing on his business and use it to promote his music. There was no way he would stop his hard work until he reached his goal. He was going to the top and nobody could stop him.

Chapter 13
How Business Was Conducted

"Successful business men always have secrets."

After a few months in the business of booking artists, Necterr figured out a way to launder drug money. He had seen hundreds of contracts and millions of dollars transferred from bank to bank and account to account. He told himself that this would be a good idea for his drug business as well. It would help things run more smoothly and reduce his risk of getting caught. Plus it was something new for him to try, and he imagined it would enable him to grow his business even more.

He took the drug and street language and his drug deals and turned them into promotional and booking lingo. Certain artists would be a certain weight, and it didn't take long for him to get the word out to the people he knew would want to do business with him. In drug slang, every drug has its price and drug dealers knew that. So Necterr became the bank to a lot of drug dealers. They quickly learned to trust him if they hadn't already, and he knew that his process was foolproof.

Even though he was out of the weed business and had nothing to do with cocaine or any other types of drugs, he began to help launder money for a lot of the dealers from state to state. As his business grew and his name got out there more and more, dealers wanted his help because they knew he was very good at what he did.

Every artist had his price. This was before Lil Wayne was a superstar, and his show price was still low. Necterr often used him in the deals. Lil Wayne knew about it but wasn't involved in these deals. He was fine with Necterr using his name as long as he kept everything looking legit and clean and didn't cause any problems for him. Soon Necterr often found himself being the middleman for two dealers trying to do business across the country from each other. He would also be the one to transport the supply.

Necterr had put a lot of thought into how to run this business, and he had a very smooth operation in place. He had a partner who worked as his manager, and he was still the DJ. His manager's name was CJ. His job was to make the whole deal sound like a concert booking. So when a drug dealer would call and say, "We want to book Lil Wayne and DJ Necterr," his manager would tell that dealer to e-mail them an offer. Sometimes, when making these drug deals, they did actual concerts. They would pay a little extra and bring Lil Wayne down and do concerts just to confuse people or see if anyone was paying close attention. For smaller deals, he would use Juelz Santana.

DJ Necterr

The responses they would get after asking for an offer were pretty amazing. They were usually something like thirty, forty, or fifty thousand for one appearance. Sometimes they would get a really great offer for two hundred thousand or more for several dates for the same artist or a combination of artists.

The artists always got their deposits up front. So the dealers would send half the money, which would be the actual drug deal. Then, when the time came for the concert, they would just cancel the show for all types of reasons. There were a few complaints when shows were cancelled, but never anything major that Necterr needed to worry about.

Necterr had a tour bus, and that was how they transferred the drugs. They would use wire transfer, bank checks, and real names to handle the money. This helped them avoid bad drug deals, setups, violence, and murders. This was a very innovative, safe, and efficient way to do business.

Previously, no one could do business within the drug trade and involve wire transfers, banks, or even checks. Necterr was the first drug dealer to turn the drug trade and do it this way. No more hotel meetings with big briefcases full of money. Now it was only cashier's checks and bank wires. This was all done with his booking company as a front. His system was working so well, he felt like some kind of genius for coming up with it.

If someone wanted weight, he gave them artists with contracts, night club venues, dates, and shows as a code. It always just looked like a promoter wanting an artist set up for a concert. It never looked like a drug deal to someone looking at it from the outside. This is what made it so perfect and foolproof.

Necterr rarely ever met another dealer face to face; nor did he ever touch money that any other dealer had touched. He always used clean bank money. This helped him avoid getting into unsafe situations like he had in the past. It also erased any trails that the authorities could possibly trace.

Knowing that some of his closest friends were not in the drug business and were not even close to being considered "gangster," Necterr had to keep his work a secret. This wasn't always easy for him to do. He didn't want to lie to his friends, but what choice did he have? Some of them would have no interest in being in the business, and others just wouldn't be able to handle it. He also had some friends who were good at a lot of other things, but just wouldn't be good in this type of business. Keeping it a secret was also another step to prevent him from being caught, so he knew that was what he needed to do no matter how difficult it might be.

Sometimes deals went bad. Since it was so hard to get drug dealers to do it this way at first, people tried to find other ways to steal money. Since Necterr's deals involved contracts and concert information, and since Lil Wayne was starting to become more popular, people started faking them out. Necterr had actual ties to the camp, so if they said they knew him and could get an actual contract from his manager, then they could start hustling people out of money.

There were also times where false drug deals were made, and money was transferred from real concert promoters really expecting Lil Wayne and DJ Necterr. Sometimes they were able to clear things up before it got bad, but if they couldn't at that time, Necterr really didn't care. He still felt untouchable and just told everyone else that it was their problem, and they would have to deal with it. He knew he might be making some enemies once again, but these weren't people he'd have to worry about. He'd dealt with much worse in the past.

While his business was thriving, his personal life was suffering, although he didn't feel as if it was at the time. He was completely into the lifestyle and having fun, but he didn't really have any great close personal relationships. He told himself he didn't need them, and most of the time, he truly believed it. He was so busy with his business and making new connections that it didn't bother him too much anyway. He actually didn't even notice it until looking back at it later on.

He did almost let himself get close to someone once, and it was all because of an accident. One day, Necterr was running late for an appointment. As he was on the way to his car, he ran directly into a woman who was out walking her dog. Actually, it looked like her dog was walking her. She was a little over five feet tall and couldn't have weighed more than ninety-eight pounds, and she was being led around by a huge Siberian husky. It was rare to see such a big dog in the area; most women he saw walking dogs had those little yappy miniature things, and half the time they were carrying them around in their purses or bags rather than walking them.

The collision had caused the bag she was carrying over her shoulder to go flying and spill out all over the ground. Though he was in a hurry, Necterr apologized and bent down to help her gather the papers that were starting to scatter in the breeze. She held tightly to the leash as her impatient dog tried to keep going, and then she bent down to help him. She apologized and said it had been all her fault, and looked up at him with the bluest eyes he had ever seen.

This woman was very pretty, with flowing blonde hair and curves in all the right places, but she didn't act like she knew it the way most of the women he met at the clubs did. She smiled and revealed her dimples, which only added to her attractiveness. She was dressed in running shorts and a T-shirt, and appeared to have little or no make-up on. He was surprised at how appealing he found this to be, since he was used to seeing women in their tight short dresses and heavy make-up.

Once the mess was cleaned up, Necterr picked up the bag and handed it to her. He introduced himself, and she thanked him and said her name was Samantha, but most people called her Sam.

Sam didn't seem to have any idea who he was, and he loved that. It was refreshing. He asked for her number and to his surprise, she hesitated, nervously explaining that she didn't usually give her number out to strangers. He convinced her that he would be the sweetest stranger she had ever met, and she gave in. As he entered it into his phone, he felt something he hadn't in a long time, a spark. He wondered if she felt it too. He thought he could tell by her radiant smile and the look in her eyes that she did, but he wasn't sure if he was just being overly confident.

That night, Necterr stumbled into his bedroom at four a.m. He wasn't sure if he was unstable because of the alcohol he'd consumed or from exhaustion. He wanted to call Sam. He'd been surrounded by beautiful ladies all night long, most of whom would have loved to come home with him, but he had resisted. He convinced himself that he also needed to resist calling her for the first time at four a.m. She didn't seem like the type of girl that would be too happy about that.

DJ Necterr

When he finally did have some time a few days later, he called Sam. He learned that she was from a small town in Illinois and had moved to California to pursue her career. She was an editor for a publishing company and worked all kinds of crazy hours depending on their needs. He told her a few things about himself too, but he was guarded and careful not to tell her too much; he didn't want her to know what his real business involved, or too much about his past. He was afraid he might scare her away, and he wasn't ready to do that just yet.

He couldn't believe it when he hung up and looked at the time on his cell. They had been talking for two hours straight, and he felt like it had been a half hour at the most. It seemed like the connection he had felt wasn't purely physical. It couldn't be if they could talk for that long during their first conversation. Most of the women he'd been with during the last few years could barely hold a ten-minute conversation with him. They had been interested in his money and in having a good time. He already knew this girl was different, and he wasn't sure how he felt about it.

After that first phone call, they started talking every day. Necterr tried to squeeze in calls and texts to her whenever he could. She would always text him back or return his calls, but she never called him first. She made it clear that she wouldn't be the one pursuing him. This was, again, an approach he wasn't used to from a woman.

It took two or three weeks of them getting to know each other on the phone before Sam was ready to actually go out with him. Because of their crazy schedules, it ended up being a Tuesday night. Necterr took her out for dinner to a fancy restaurant. They shared a bottle of wine and some great conversation. Just as their time on the phone always did, their time together flew by. As they were leaving, Necterr noticed other men at the bar looking at Sam. She was dressed in a simple, modest black dress and again wore little make-up, but he clearly wasn't imagining how naturally stunning she was.

Normally Necterr would assume that they would go back to his house for a long night of drinks and sex, but he didn't want to do that this time with this girl. He figured he probably could have lured her in since she was tipsy from the wine, but he didn't want to. He drove her home, and they sat in his car for another forty-five minutes, their first kiss lasting almost that long. When she got out, she smiled and told him to call her when he had time. Though he thought about it often and even dialed the number a few times, Necterr didn't call her.

He was getting busier and busier and knew he didn't have time to get involved with Sam. He figured even talking to her on the phone would make him want to see her again, and he didn't think that was a good idea. He didn't have time, she probably wouldn't approve of his business, and he had no desire to put her in any kind of danger. Even if this wasn't likely, there was always a chance. He worked hard to push her out of his mind and hoped she wouldn't call him. He also hoped that she had just forgotten about him, and that he hadn't hurt her feelings.

As the weeks wore on and his business grew and grew, Necterr started feeling very confident again. Though he had many chances to get into relationships with beautiful and seemingly great women, he chose not to. He stuck to his pattern of one-night stands, strip clubs, and high-class prostitutes. That way he could have some fun without any strings attached. He would never say it out loud, but it was also the only way he felt he could avoid being hurt by a woman again. He didn't have the time or patience to go through that again. He spent his time with his business associates, friends that he had to keep his secret from, and on his own. He kept telling himself that he liked things that way.

During that time of his life, Necterr's parents had decided to move to Italy to enjoy life. That had always been their dream, and he was able to send them there to live. It felt really good for him to use his money to finally do something great for them. Plus, he felt it was safer for them to be out of the area and the country. He knew that in his business, he couldn't be too careful in protecting his loved ones.

While in Italy, Necterr's dad found a job doing what he loved, as the head coach of a baseball team. Necterr didn't talk much to his dad at that time because he was always working. Plus there were the time differences, which made it really hard to coordinate schedules so they could have uninterrupted time to talk. He was glad that his father was finally able to work doing something he really enjoyed, and felt like he had finally done something to help him by putting him in that right place at the right time. It felt great to be helping him instead of hurting or worrying him for once.

Necterr still had a pretty good relationship with his mom, but he only got to talk to her on the phone maybe one time per week. It gave him relief and pride to hear the happiness and peacefulness in her voice. He felt she deserved some peace in her life after everything she'd been through with him. He was glad he could finally make some of it up to her too. He felt a little lonely each time they hung up; sometimes he missed that family connection that so many other people seemed to have.

Because of his business he didn't really get together with family to celebrate birthdays or holidays too much, and sometimes that brought him down a little. The payoff was that now he had been able to do something for his parents that they never would have been able to afford on their own. He could also sleep better at night knowing they were completely safe if anything went wrong.

Although some people might have accused him of being a horrible son and sibling, his intentions for his family had always been good. He wanted to be able to keep them safe and take care of them. He wanted them to be financially secure and able to live out the rest of their lives having fun rather than working at jobs they hated just to pay the bills. He wanted that for everyone in his family. It was a big part of the reason he did what he did. They didn't realize it, but maybe someday they would.

Necterr also hoped and believed that someday they would all spend time together again as a happy family. This was something he looked forward to in the distant future, once he had really made his fortune and a name for himself in the music industry. He pictured them all sitting around the dinner table toasting each other and laughing about the trouble he'd caused in his younger years. His parents would go around the table bragging about the talents of each of their children, and he'd finally be included. He pictured his siblings with their spouses next to them and kids running around. They'd all spend the night drinking and telling stories from the past. He could almost hear his music playing in the background of this imagined scene.

In reality, this was around the time his nephew was born. Necterr knew his brother still loved him, but they didn't have much of a relationship anymore. He believed that his brother had figured out what was really going on. He probably believed that he had to choose between keeping his family safe and maintaining a close relationship with Necterr. Knowing of his little brother's troubles, he had gone to great lengths to distance himself. Necterr didn't get to see much of him or have the chance to bond with his new baby nephew. He really couldn't blame his brother, though. He probably would have handled the situation the same way if the roles had been reversed.

In his head, Necterr's music career was going well, and he believed that like his parents, he was doing what he enjoyed. Actually, though, his music career was at a standstill. He was around all of these artists doing a lot of work, but it had nothing to do with being musical or entertaining. Instead of working alongside these artists as a fellow performer, he was just a dealer and a connection, but he wouldn't admit that to himself at the time. His business was thriving, but once again he had gotten sidetracked. He was wasting precious time. His real talents that he knew he had been born to share with the world were going unused once again.

DJ Necterr

Necterr worked hard to block out negative thoughts and continue running his business. He never felt in danger of being caught. He knew that he had finally come up with the best and most fail-proof idea ever. There was no way he could possibly get caught, but he never took any chances and continued to watch his back.

DJ Necterr

Chapter 14
What About My Friends?

Necterr had a number of questionable friends who did nothing but pry by asking a lot of questions. These friends wanted to know exactly what he was doing as well as how he was doing it. As he was still trying to keep his business a secret, he found their questioning to be very annoying and somewhat troublesome. His theory remained that no one could tell on him if they didn't know anything, and he wanted to keep it that way.

One of his closest friends, who was and still is just nosy by nature, tried really hard to figure out his extravagant lifestyle. There were also constant questions about all of the traveling that he was doing. Necterr figured out that it didn't take much to distract him, though. All he had to do was offer to take him to a strip club and pay for some woman to come back to the room, and the conversation would change immediately. He'd learned to use this strategy with this friend and a few others early on.

One time, Necterr went to the casino with about twenty-five thousand dollars, and that was very awkward for one of his friends to see. This friend didn't say anything at the time, but Necterr knew that he had big questions. It was obvious by the way he looked at the money and at him every time he took out a big stack of cash.

Unfortunately, Necterr lost every penny of the money within an hour playing blackjack. This wasn't unfortunate because he carried a lot since by this time he had plenty of money to burn. The unfortunate part was that it made his friend even more wary. When Necterr didn't get frustrated or upset about his loss, the friend he was with became extremely suspicious, and this made the situation even more awkward. This friend had more of an attitude than Necterr did when he lost, but it didn't bother Necterr. What seemed to bother his friend even more was when Necterr made a stop at a weird hotel and went in for about ten minutes. When he came back out, he told him that they were headed back to the casino. His friend was confused, but thought maybe Necterr was hungry and wanted to use the free food comps he had gotten since he'd already lost all of his money.

Necterr gave his friend five hundred dollars and told him to meet back up with him in the lobby in an hour. His friend walked away with no questions asked. Whether he was still confused and suspicious didn't seem to matter when Necterr was giving him money. When they met after the hour was up, he saw Necterr with a new backpack filled so full it was bulging. He figured out that it was full of money and commented on it even though Necterr hadn't shown him. This was when the questions really started to come. "What do you actually do? How did you get that? Did you rob a bank?" His questions bombarded Necterr like bullets one after another.

His friend was very confused and very curious. Necterr continued to do what he had to in order to keep from telling him the truth. Finally, it got so bad that Necterr tried to avoid him. The more distant he tried to be with the guy, the more the friend wanted to hang out with him. The sad thing was Necterr could tell that he was trying to figure out what was going on and why Necterr wouldn't tell him, and that was his sole purpose for wanting to hang out so often.

These situations popped up all of the time with all of his friends. It was uncomfortable for Necterr, but not for them. He was continuously getting them anything and everything they could possibly want or need, so they were coming out on the winning end of the situation. When he felt uncomfortable, Necterr used his money to distract them and, in turn, cover up his discomfort. Amazingly, most of these friendships weren't negatively impacted by his secret at all. Everything stayed pretty much the same except for a few extreme cases where he had to cut ties with certain people.

Necterr knew that, with the increasing amount of money that he was making and the life that he was living, it would get harder and harder to continue to hide his business. One time, a deposit was made, and he made up a story to his friend that the money came from a scam that he had pulled. He didn't go into detail on what kind of scam it was; he didn't have to. He just told his friend that he had learned about it through one of his African friends who had shown him the ropes on how to make money fast by scamming people. That was enough information for that friend at that time.

Necterr didn't enjoy lying to his friends, but he wasn't about to get caught because somebody else couldn't keep their mouth shut. The scam story felt like a safe one to Necterr because it made him feel that if for some reason that friend would ever be in a situation where he could get out of jail by saying something to someone about Necterr, it would be that he was a scam artist.

Scam artists do easy federal time, so this was preferable to getting put away for major drug trafficking. It was the perfect front to use with his friends while he continued to conduct business. He had them all fooled and in the meantime, business started getting even better. He took great care of his friends and treated them extremely well. He took them on extravagant trips to Miami, Vegas, and Mexico. The favorite spot was Vegas, though, with its huge variety of casinos and strip clubs. His friends loved it there.

DJ Necterr

CJ, one of Necterr's good friends, and his "cousin" (they always said they were cousins, but really weren't), Ramon, were always with him at this time. They went to Vegas to celebrate New Year's. Necterr took not only CJ and Ramon, but also the whole crew and all of their friends. Necterr ended up booking an entire floor at three different hotels for all of these people. He had the suites, and the homies had the regular rooms.

Necterr's suite on that trip was one of the best he'd ever stayed in. It was the perfect spot to party with everyone. It was four thousand square feet with a suspended walkway leading up to it. Inside the suite was a beautiful indoor fountain surrounded by a flower garden. A huge fireplace was a feature in the living room and both of the master bedrooms. Off of the master bedrooms were floor to ceiling glass sliding doors which led out to a beautiful outdoor terrace and a solarium. Of course there was a fifty-inch plasma in the living room complete with its own home theater system and slightly smaller thirty-inch televisions to match in every other room. Necterr's favorite feature was the L-shaped bar made entirely of sparkling emerald colored glass. Each bathroom had its own whirlpool tub and steam shower, and Necterr smiled as he imagined the crazy things that would go on in those rooms each night. He was ready to have some fun with his friends and business associates.

DJ Necterr

Necterr made sure that this trip was full of women, sex, and drugs for everyone involved, including himself. He was definitely ready to relax and let go of the stress of running his business for a few days. It was New Year's Eve week. Not only was he in Vegas at one of the wildest times of the year, but he was there with the whole team. They threw a huge party in his suite on the first night.

Necterr knew no party would be complete without strippers, so he hired a few of them to keep himself and his guests entertained and busy. They had security at each end of the hall where the elevator was, so that nobody they didn't want around could find their way to his suite. For the most part, they were open to meeting new people if they seemed like they were just looking for a good time. They must have sounded like they were having fun because some strangers found their way in, after being totally cleared by security, and partied with them all night.

Necterr always had money on his mind, so he charged outsiders to come and see the women dance and get naked. If they wanted to have sex with a girl, he provided that too, for the right price. Of course this wasn't difficult to get the strippers to do, and after some of the ladies who weren't strippers had a few drinks, they were ready to do the same. Necterr figured that being a boss meant he could still make money in all different ways, especially within the confines of his own hotel suite.

They tore the hotel rooms up from top to bottom. When Necterr woke up the next morning in a fog, he found that he had a gorgeous naked woman on each side of him. He grinned, wishing he could remember what had happened when he finally made it to bed in the early morning hours. He realized that grinning only made his head hurt worse, so he stopped. He had to stumble over passed-out bodies, some clothed and some not so much. There was broken glass everywhere. Various undergarments hung from lamps and ceiling fans, and the plush white carpeting was many different colors now; Necterr didn't even want to imagine what substances had caused the stains. He was feeling a little queasy and tried to focus on getting himself a glass of water. He spotted his cell lying in a puddle of something on the counter and quickly grabbed it, hoping it wasn't fried. It appeared to be working, so he scrolled through his missed texts and calls. Most of them were from business associates, and his mom had called earlier the night before. He made a mental note to call her back as soon as he got back home. The next number was slightly familiar, but he had to struggle to recall whose it was. He shook his head swiftly, trying to snap out of his hangover, and realized it was Sam's number. He backtracked to a text he'd skipped over from the same number. The message was nothing but three question marks. He wasn't sure what mental note to make about Sam, so he vowed to avoid thinking about her until his trip was over. He couldn't even imagine what she might think of this scene which began with him crawling out of a king-size bed where two high-class strippers were sleeping. He looked around at the devastated kitchen and then peered into the dining room.

When he spotted the extravagant dining room table, he noticed that all of its twelve chairs were missing. Then he noticed a sparkling pile of glass near the large window that overlooked the city and wondered why he hadn't seen the gaping hole in it before. Reluctantly, he walked to the window and looked out and down. He laughed out loud to himself as he spotted the broken chairs. A few had smashed down onto a parked car and the rest lay in pieces on the sidewalk. Necterr wondered if he was still high. Would there be any other explanation for his finding this so funny?

Of course it didn't take long for hotel management to figure out where the chairs had come from and force their way into the suite. Necterr and his friends were politely asked to leave and told there would be no further questions asked or charges for the damage if they did so quickly and quietly.

By the third night of the trip, they were in their third hotel. Necterr decided when he was only slightly buzzed to give a speech about his guests respecting hotel property. He started out seriously, but couldn't seem to keep a straight face halfway through it. Someone turned up the music and he whipped his martini glass against the wall, causing everyone holding a glass to do the same.

To this day, Necterr still can't stay at these hotels, but his friends still talk about that trip, and he knows they'll never forget it. People say money can't buy happiness, but knowing he'd bought these memories for his friends made Necterr extremely happy.

Necterr was a good friend to have, and all of his friends knew it. He got the girls, paid car notes, and got his friends anything else they could possibly want or need. Business started getting so good that the bank would not let him take out all of his money for each deal. This was a problem that could have really hindered his business, so he decided he had to finally involve his friends in the process. He now needed their help to keep things running smoothly. His first step was to change his business name from Legacy Booking to Legacy Enterprises.

Now that he had truly tasted success, he was addicted to it and wanted more. He didn't need any more money; he had more than he knew what to do with. Still, he had to become a bigger business, and to do that, he would need to let other people be involved in the receipt and handling of the money. He was an enterprise, and his friends were the business. Therefore, he could still monitor all of the money coming in and out. It would just come to their accounts, they would make the deposits and withdrawals, and he would collect.

This was the sweetest setup he had ever had. All he had to do was sit back and watch his bank account flow. He would occasionally show up at different cities as a DJ and make radio drops for promoters, but that wasn't like work for him anyway; that was fun.

When the time came for him to explain the plan to his friends, it was easy. All he had to do was ask one question: "Y'all want to live like me?"

Of course the answer was yes. Then all he had to do was show them what the process was and give them a few simple steps to follow. All they really needed to do was call CJ. With CJ and Necterr on the contract, they could do anything. It took only a few weeks for them to get the process down, and only months for them to become successful. Necterr realized that he finally trusted his friends, although part of the trust probably came from the fact that he still felt invincible.

None of Necterr's friends turned on him, but they did go behind his back sometimes and do faulty deals. Necterr's and CJ's names were attached to every deal. That wasn't the worst part, though; his account was also attached to every deal.

This meant that Necterr's reputation and financial reputation with the banks would take the fall when faulty deals were made. When someone did a faulty deal with a legitimate person, they didn't care and weren't worried because they were part of an army full of gangsters. They wouldn't worry about anybody doing anything about it because they knew that nobody would have the courage to stand up to them.

This was around the time when Lil Wayne started showing up in the news for no-show after no-show. Necterr wasn't sure if this was due to his crew being greedy, but he had a crazy feeling that it was, and so did Lil Wayne. Necterr wasn't happy about this, but he figured it was bound to happen when other people got involved with his business.

As a result of the suspicions he had regarding Necterr's crew, Lil Wayne stopped getting drugs from them and started to deal with another drug dealer from Los Angeles. His name won't be mentioned here, but he was and still is used a lot in the music business.

Necterr then took a huge and somewhat risky step. He employed over two hundred of his friends under his business license. He had his bank write checks to a number of these friends. He let them cash the checks and keep twenty percent of each check. He was the perfect drug dealer.

One time they had a big deal that resulted in about two hundred fifty thousand dollars deposited. Necterr felt uncomfortable about having that much in the account. He decided to take out at least one hundred fifty thousand dollars. To do so he had to write checks to fifteen people of nine thousand five hundred dollars each. He wouldn't forget the looks on most of their faces as long as he lived as he handed them those checks. It was unforgettable and priceless to be able to hand them that money. He even wrote checks to some friends who weren't part of the business. As long as they were receiving money, they didn't ask too many questions. They must have thought Necterr was the most generous guy on earth. They also still got their twenty percent, so this was a deal that helped a lot of his friends out all in one day, and it helped him make his account seem more realistic.

Necterr was running a creative and lucrative business, taking good care of some of his family and his friends, and having a great time. He didn't see a limit to the amount of money he could make or the fun he could have. The uneasiness he had felt about letting anyone know what he was doing was gone. His friends were doing an okay job, and he was a true pro now. Nothing would stop him. He didn't even care that he had sidestepped his real dream again. Or he just didn't realize it yet.

Chapter 15
The Perfect Drug Dealer

Necterr was the perfect drug dealer at this time. There were hundreds of thousands of dollars made each month, and there was no sign at all that business would be slowing down any time soon. In fact, it was just the opposite; business was growing at an unbelievable rate. He had no obvious ties to the drug business, so his position was virtually risk free. He had his friends working for and with him, and his business was running like a well-oiled machine. He felt like he had reached the top once again, and nothing and nobody could bring him down.

He didn't have any major or specific problems with his friends, but Necterr was starting to notice that some of them were getting extremely greedy. They tried to make more money on certain deals and didn't seem to care at all about pissing off their customers. Sometimes Necterr had to remind them that they were working on behalf of him and his name.

Others were starting to act like they might be jealous of him and his position, although they had no real reason to be. He treated them all so well that he believed they had nothing to complain about. Some of them did complain, though, and seemed a little bitter toward him when the subject of how much money he was making came up. Of course, they were the ones who always brought this subject up. He was too smart to bring up his finances with them. He figured out that maybe the more they had, the more they would always want, since that was how he had felt. Maybe this was just human nature. He didn't want any trouble, so he closely watched the ones that needed watching.

Since he had started in the drug business several years before, Necterr had been arrested several times. Sometimes he was arrested for doing really stupid things like smoking weed in a parked car in a red zone. He knew this was a very stupid thing to do, but he didn't care about the tickets. It was nothing to pay a parking ticket, and he really wouldn't have cared if he got one every day for the rest of his life. He didn't realize the cops would be assholes and actually arrest him the first time it happened, or he might have thought twice about parking there. Just as it seemed to have been all of his life, those in authority always seemed threatened by him and never gave him much of a chance. Little did they know how much authority and power Necterr actually had.

Many of the times he was arrested were the result of being in the wrong place at the wrong time. He was a very strong-willed person, and if a cop asked him a question, he would be a dick to them and never answer the question being asked. He would respond with a huge attitude every time. He simply didn't have time for their shit, and if they were going to inconvenience him, he would make the experience as unpleasant for them as possible. He would have to answer every question they had with a smartass response such as, "Ask your mom!" That's when they would arrest him and charge him with obstruction of justice. He'd just give them a cocky smile as they cuffed him and shoved him into their car. He knew all too well that he would be released the next morning.

After a while, he knew it would always be just one simple night in jail, so it almost became like a game to him. He would get arrested outside of clubs or outside of girls' houses after the clubs. He always played it cool and acted like it was no big deal even though some of the ladies seemed a little shocked when the squad cars pulled up. Necterr knew he would get out in the morning or after three days at the very most, so these instances didn't bother him a bit.

Necterr never spent more than two days in jail during any of these times. There were numerous known testimonies because snitches talked to the Feds about him, but there was no evidence. He had his ideas about who these snitches were, but he was never completely sure. Even if he had known, his rule was to never confront a snitch as they are well protected by the law. That was what he believed anyway. Besides, he figured they weren't really worth his time, and he wasn't about to lower himself to their level and deal with them.

Necterr touched nothing and ran a booking business. The last three times he was arrested, he was released with no bail and no case pending. The authorities didn't have a clue what he was doing. His family, on the other hand, was starting to really wonder what was going on with him. They were aware of his lifestyle, and he thought they at least sensed the fact that he had been in and out of jail if they hadn't heard it directly.

Necterr's family seemed concerned for him, but they were also pretty busy with their own lives, so he didn't see them often. His parents were still in Italy. His brother was living in the south. His sister had just gotten married, so she was very focused on starting her new life with her husband. His other sister was doing her college thing, which, between classes, parties, and extracurricular activities, took up most of her time.

Necterr's mom thought that he did business with promoters. That was fine with him. He wanted her to believe he was a successful businessman. It was also his goal to make sure she could relax and not have to worry about him anymore, and her belief that he was running a lucrative business would allow her to do that.

He still didn't talk to his dad much, due to their differences in schedule; however, he sensed that his dad knew he was doing something wrong. His dad was very good at reading people, a quality Necterr must have inherited from him. Necterr knew that no matter what he thought, they had one thing in common. They had similar lifestyles at one time. His dad may not have been on the same level that he was, but he had also lived a life of crime. What could he really say about Necterr's choice of lifestyle? Necterr was truly his father's son.

His siblings were a different story. Because he was very good at reading people and knowing what was really being said even if they didn't always come right out and say it, he knew something was up with them. He could tell from certain conversations that they were concerned about him. They definitely knew that he was doing something illegal; they couldn't believe there was any other way he would be making so much money so quickly and living the fast lifestyle that he was.

Necterr's sister thought that he booked shows to drug dealers. She clearly didn't approve, not because she thought she was better than him, but because she was afraid he'd get into big trouble or hurt badly someday. She didn't hide her feelings and suspicions from him; she told him straight to his face what she thought of him and of the situation.

Since he and his brother were only a few years apart, they had many mutual friends, so word got out to him pretty quickly about the way Necterr was living. His brother had tried to piece everything he knew about Necterr together along with what he had heard about how he was living and had come to the conclusion that he must have been a scam artist. As fast as word about Necterr's life had traveled to his brother, his brother's opinions about what he was doing got back to Necterr just as quickly. He had to give him credit; it had been a good guess, and Necterr figured that in a way, his brother was right: he was a type of scam artist.

His brother thought he was pretty smart to have figured out how to do something really well and be so successful, but at the same time, he thought whatever Necterr was doing had to be high risk, and when they did talk, he tried to warn him. He was good at voicing his opinions, and actually pretty convincing at times. Necterr was hardheaded, though, so these were the times that he actually tuned him out.

His oldest sister thought that he got investors to invest in his gambling. This was something that Necterr found out from a mutual friend who knew her son's coach. He realized at that point that the gambling habit he had was probably a very good way to cover up what was really going on.

Necterr still gambles today for fun, but not like he did in those days. Looking back on those times, Necterr realizes he did have quite a gambling problem. If he made thirty grand in a day, there were times he would take that money and keep on going. He wouldn't be able to quit until he had lost it all in the same day. He didn't even try to stop himself; he knew it was just money to play with, and he had plenty of it to spare.

Many days, he would wake up unable to think about anything but gambling. After doing the things he needed to do, he couldn't go home until he hit up the casino. Everyone at just about every casino from Cali to Vegas knew him on a first-name basis, and he knew them.

Necterr knew them, and they knew all of his habits, and they did whatever they needed to do to cater to him. They even knew the constant cycle of girls he would bring with him. Although he did have plenty of women to take with him to the casinos, he tried to keep them somewhat consistent to make things easier. Whenever he booked a room, they automatically knew to book an extra room for him. This was in case he wanted to take a break from his original female date and hang with someone new for a while. They knew how he was and had no problem with it. In fact, he was pretty sure that most of them admired and maybe even envied him. They treated him like a king.

So far, in his short lifetime, Necterr had made way over a million dollars and hadn't paid any taxes. Needless to say, he ran into some small tax problems when he started reporting this huge income and wasn't paying any taxes. He knew the

IRS expected their money, but he didn't care. He felt that the IRS was just another company or business, not the government. He couldn't see any reason why he should pay any company that hadn't put anything at all into his business.

He had to meet with the IRS to discuss this problem and covered most of it up with his gambling problem. To divert their attention he told them that the money came from gambling, and they seemed to believe that, which was all he really cared about. He didn't need them or anyone else digging around for additional information about where and how he made his money.

A highlight in Necterr's life at this time was that he finally got to meet his second nephew. His brother's new son was just a baby, but it was still great to be able to see him. Necterr knew that he and his brother were still the best of friends even though they didn't see each other much or see eye to eye. They were just two totally different people. Necterr realized and respected this difference, and he was so grateful to be a part of his nephew's life.

One of the worst things that happened around this time in his life was that one of the ladies Necterr was messing with said she was pregnant. He immediately believed she was just seeing the dollar signs. He didn't trust her. He couldn't believe that she was really pregnant, or if she was, not by him.

Necterr wouldn't have minded having a baby, especially since he had just spent some time with his brother's kid. What bothered him was that he was pretty sure he didn't want her baby. Not being sure it was his made the situation even more frustrating. He didn't have the time or energy to be getting all excited about having a kid of his own just to find out that it wasn't his.

Necterr told this girl that he would be happy to be there for her and for the child, as long as when the baby was born, a blood test would be done first thing. She tried to fight that notion, claiming that he didn't deserve to be around his own baby if that was all he was worried about. To Necterr, that was a very bad sign. Then, not even a month later, she disappeared.

A short while later, she called and left a message on his voicemail, claiming that she was having twins. She left no number or contact information, which Necterr thought was strange. Necterr wondered if he had made a mistake and should put some effort into finding her. He knew it would be his right to still insist on the blood test.

He tried to forget about it, but that didn't work too well. Finally, he did some research and found her on the Internet. He was shocked to see that she was as skinny as ever and not pregnant at all. Then he found out that she had miscarried.

Necterr was heartbroken because he knew that he had the twin gene in his family. When he finally tracked her down and talked to her, she said she had miscarried only one baby. She was so sad and depressed about the first baby that she had then aborted the second. Necterr felt terrible. He wished he had been there for her, thinking that maybe then she would have kept the second baby. They resumed their friendship after that and worked through the difficult time together. They vowed to keep in touch, and Necterr even put her through college when she was ready. The two of them are still friends to this day, and Shania is currently working at getting her PhD.

Necterr was still DJing, but he had slowed way down. He made his appearances in order to stay connected, but he had completely lost his focus. It was hard for him to make an appearance as a DJ for five hundred dollars when he knew he could make twenty thousand a night at the casino. He was also very busy with his business and almost looked at DJing as a waste of his time. He still made frequent appearances at concerts and parties because those were the events that were the most fun. He also knew he could do business at the same time, so it was always a win-win situation for him to attend these events.

It was at one of those parties that Necterr met a woman named Ashley Mitchell. Ashley was the personal assistant for a rapper named Memphis Bleek. Necterr liked Ashley and became instant friends with her. They spent a lot of time talking on the phone. After she got to know him, she said she was going to get him inside Jay-Z's label. Memphis Bleek was Jay-Z's hype man, good friend, and an artist on his label. This was the perfect connection for Necterr at this time, so he figured it would be smart to milk his friendship with Ashley Mitchell. It was a quick and easy way to get inside the hottest rap label around.

While this was in the works, Necterr was mostly having fun spending his money as fast as he could. He was still taking care of those that he cared about, but he had the system working so well that his friends did most of the work for him, while he sat back and enjoyed the benefits. He continued making and working new connections and living the good life.

One night, Necterr was out with his boys at one of their favorite strip clubs. He walked into the club and noticed a beautiful dancer who immediately started paying a lot of attention to him. Her name was Vivica, and she was a porn star. He didn't know that she was porn star when he met her, though; he found this out much later.

She told him, when they talked after that first night, that when he had walked into the club, she could sense his swag and boss-like mannerisms, and she knew at that moment that she had to have him. Necterr was used to not showing too much interest to a woman, but it was difficult for him with this one. This was a lady who knew exactly what she wanted, and Necterr had the feeling that she pretty much always found a way to get it.

What got him when they first met was that she paid for everything at the strip club. She bought his drinks and bought his bottle. He was very surprised by this. He had become used to being the one who took care of everyone else. Nobody had offered to do anything financially for him since Jerome had died. Vivica had him hooked on day one, not only because she was sexy, gorgeous, and entertaining to be with, but also because he knew she didn't want to be around him for his money. She clearly didn't need it. They started spending a lot of time together, and Necterr realized quickly that she might be the perfect woman for him, the perfect drug dealer.

Chapter 16
On the Run Again

Oh no! He fucked up again. It was August of 2007, and he thought that he was going to be richer than he had ever been. Although he was living well, he wanted more money and power and was always looking for new opportunities to advance his position. One such opportunity appeared to come out of nowhere. Necterr met the biggest Ecstasy dealer in Nevada, and little did he know that this chance meeting would have a huge and devastating impact on his life.

Necterr was at one of his favorite casinos playing blackjack. He was playing very large hands, as he usually did, and sometimes that attracted the attention of others. He was used to drawing attention to himself as he played; in fact, he had grown to like the attention and the way other players would look at him in awe. One other player in particular seemed to really be watching him. Since he had started playing very large hands, this other guy at the table really took notice and struck up a conversation with him.

This guy seemed pretty cool at first, even though he lost a bunch of money at the table where they met. Like Necterr, he didn't react much when he lost, which showed Necterr that money was not an issue for him. He looked to be about twenty years older than Necterr and was very mellow and friendly. They talked mainly about blackjack that night, but Necterr figured out quickly that he was probably talking to someone very powerful and important in the Vegas scene. He knew if he played his cards right, this could turn into a very important friendship for him.

The guy invited Necterr up to a hotel party, where he introduced him to some nice young ladies. These ladies were probably high-class prostitutes, but Necterr couldn't be sure. He didn't have to pay anything out of his pocket, but he was pretty sure they were probably on this guy's payroll. Necterr didn't care either way; he had learned to take full advantage of every situation that was presented to him, and beautiful ladies were no exception to this rule. He had a great time with them while he contemplated what his next move might be with this powerful new acquaintance.

Ironically, this guy was called Black Jack. Black Jack was a very good and well-known businessman in the state of Nevada. He was very relevant in the night club scene and invested in a lot of the smaller Las Vegas promoters. Always thinking about how to improve business, Necterr decided he had met Black Jack for a reason and couldn't pass up the opportunity to take advantage of the situation.

Luckily for Necterr, he had a female who was so much in love with him that she would do anything he asked her to do. He put this woman to work on Black Jack's right-hand man. She willingly seduced him and got him to open up to her about his life and his role in Black Jack's business. It didn't take her long to hook Necterr up with this guy. She used her power of seduction to get him to trust and talk to Necterr, which was exactly what he had hoped would happen. Once he started talking to Necterr, he revealed information about Black Jack's business, including details about all of his connections and everyone that he dealt with.

Necterr and his crew quickly convinced Black Jack's right-hand man to work for them and set up deals with Black Jack's customers for a fraction of the price. All Necterr had to do was offer this guy a small percentage into the business, and with that offer came more power. Even though Black Jack could probably offer him the same type of deals, Necterr had an advantage—his connections with and exposure to the celebrities.

Black Jack was also around celebrities, but he never saw a reason to put his right-hand man around them. Necterr noticed right away that this guy was the type who loved to be in the limelight, and he would totally be into the celebrity scene. This was how Necterr completely won him over. He made him like a local celebrity to all of his friends, and this guy started having his own little groupies. This was the key. He was a sucker for easy women, and Necterr made that happen for him. He was used to Black Jack keeping him happy with high-class prostitutes, but Necterr kept him happy with women he would never have gotten, not even with money. Necterr and his crew had quickly and easily convinced Black Jack's right-hand man to come and work for and with them.

After setting this up, they took over the state of Nevada. It did not take long for Black Jack to figure out that his business was being stolen right from under his feet. He knew he had lost his right-hand man to Necterr and that Necterr was behind his losing business. Necterr had a big army, but it was definitely not bigger than Black Jack's.

Black Jack had a whole state behind him. Not only did he have a whole state behind him, but Necterr learned that he was also backed by the Italians. This was the word on the street, and not long after Black Jack figured out what had happened, Necterr received a few strange phone calls from gentlemen with Italian accents.

As he often did at the blackjack table, Necterr had taken a very risky chance in order to gain more money and power. This time, luck was not in his favor. Necterr had pissed off the mob. These guys were nothing but scary and fearsome. Necterr knew that they didn't waste much time with warnings and threats. If someone got in their way, they made that person disappear quickly and efficiently. They were known to be the most cold-blooded people that existed and often tortured their enemies to death. He'd heard plenty of horror stories about what had happened to people who crossed these guys.

The authorities don't think the mob owns half of Vegas like they did in earlier years, but they definitely do. It may not be the casinos anymore, but the majority of the night clubs in Vegas are owned by the mob. Anyone who messes with them usually ends up disappearing or mysteriously murdered. They basically rule the city, and there aren't many brave enough to go up against them.

Over half of the night clubs and strip clubs in Vegas are run by Italians. When someone sets up a meeting to throw a big event at one of these night clubs, the meeting is always going to be with a guy with an Italian last name. Necterr had had a few meetings to set up events, and they all ended up being with an Italian general manager. This made it very difficult for Necterr to launder money in the state.

Necterr had to be very careful. He didn't believe by any means that everyone with an Italian last name was crooked. It was just that he had to be very careful with the business he was running and how shady he was being. He was stealing business, so he could never be too careful.

DJ Necterr

Within a three-month time period, Necterr had stolen most of Black Jack's business, and money was on his head again. He was very worried about his family because he knew he was dealing with the mob now. He didn't know if they operated the way he had seen them operate on television, but if they did, they would surely find and go after his family to get to him. Necterr wouldn't be able to forgive himself if his unquenchable thirst for money and success led to anyone he cared about getting hurt.

Necterr started to get phone calls that money was on his head. He also received many disturbing text messages threatening physical harm to him and anyone associated with him. Since he had a small team in Nevada, they were able to tell him what they were hearing. He didn't like what they were telling him and was starting to think he had really gotten himself in deep this time.

Necterr had a number of people looking for him. He found out that his picture was posted with security at every night club in Nevada. Security was told that he was considered a troublemaker in the club scene. It was all a front so the mob could track him down. Security was told to call the general manager if he showed up, and that was all part of their cover-up. They couldn't put it out there that they wanted to kill him, so they put it out there as a legitimate security issue, saying he was a risk to the club. He was in trouble and so was his business; he could not club anywhere in Vegas.

It was around this time that Necterr was invited to a big industry party in Vegas. It was the weekend of the MTV VMAs, and the party would be full of a number of big name artists. He had been personally invited by the artist, but when the event came up, no artists appeared; therefore, he didn't either. This was a huge disappointment to him as he had really been looking forward to the party.

It was word on the streets that anyone who attended events with him would get exactly what he got. Obviously, this was a big turnoff for celebrities and connections who didn't want to find themselves in the middle of trouble, or, even worse, dead. More and more people were starting to avoid him and any association with his name. Word had spread like fire and nobody wanted to take any chances.

Once again, Necterr was on the run. He could not show his face anywhere. This time it was more than just a regional thing. He discovered that people were looking for him from California to Chicago. Black Jack had associates everywhere. Necterr knew he had to go into major hiding to protect himself and everyone who knew him.

He took all of the money he had made and did more than lie low. He moved outside of the country for a few months. He didn't tell anyone where he was going, not even his girl. He knew this was a terribly dangerous move for his business, but what good would money do him if he was dead? He had to go somewhere where they wouldn't be able to easily find him. That place didn't exist in the United States, at least not at that time. He needed to give Black Jack and the mob some time to cool down and forget about him and what he had done to them.

Necterr didn't stay in any one place for too long; he knew he couldn't. He went down to Mexico for a few weeks. This was during the time when a passport wasn't needed to go from the U.S. to Mexico, so he would always fly to the border and then drive across. He never had any trouble crossing the border.

Once in Mexico, he found a decent hotel to live in from day to day. He didn't look for anything extravagant; he didn't want to run into anyone who might know him, and if Black Jack sent someone out of the U.S. to look for him, they'd most likely look in the nicer areas and the five star hotels first. He ate a couple of simple meals a day and kept to himself. He switched hotels every few days and was basically living out of his bag. He did his best not to draw attention to himself. Sometimes he'd join a tour group and go sightseeing with them. He figured he looked more like a tourist than a native anyway, and it was something to pass the time.

One tour involved a long trek through the Mexican countryside by bus, and Necterr couldn't believe what he saw as he gazed out the window.

He saw tiny dirty shacks lined up along the roadside, looking like their roofs were ready to cave in any minute. Filthy-faced children ran around the grassless yards, wearing tattered clothes and no shoes. He couldn't believe that there were people who actually lived like this and wondered to himself what they might do with the money he often spent on one weekend party.

One day when he was walking to his favorite restaurant for lunch, Necterr couldn't help but stop when a little shoeless boy held out his hat, begging for money. Necterr reached into his pocket and pulled out a handful of pesos. He tossed them into the hat and watched the young boy's eyes light up with gratitude and awe. He couldn't believe how much the boy appreciated a few pesos. Before he knew it, Necterr had a trail of raggedy children following him down the sidewalk. They had seen him give the young boy money and hoped they could get some too. He realized he had made a mistake and avoided looking at them. He ducked into a darkly lit bar and sighed with guilty relief, knowing they couldn't follow him in without shoes on their feet. He wondered how long they would wait for him to come out as he ordered his first drink.

Necterr had also seen and partied in a few mansions while in Mexico, and he realized that there was a very prominent and powerful upper class, and a very poverty-stricken lower class. What baffled him was that the middle class seemed nonexistent. A few people seemed to have all of the money, and they were the drug dealers and politicians. The poor lived right there among them, and it didn't seem to bother them one bit to walk right by the starving children who sold gum on the city sidewalks. Necterr decided that when he got his business up and running again, he'd find a way to donate to the poor in Mexico. It was something easy he could do to make a difference. It also occurred to him that if he thought about it, he could easily write some great lyrics about the ridiculous distribution of wealth that he had witnessed. He hadn't done any writing in a while and decided he really missed it.

His lifestyle had changed drastically. The pace was much slower. He didn't really do any major partying. He did drink a lot, since he didn't have much else to do, but didn't do any other drugs. He didn't have any real friends or girls. He would occasionally hook up with a tourist, but didn't even do that very often. When he did, he had to be secretive or dishonest about who he was and what he did for a living as well as what he was doing in Mexico. He was suspicious of every single person he talked to no matter how innocent he or she seemed. He knew the fewer real personal connections he made, the safer he would be. Many of his days he spent walking around taking in the sights or lying in a hammock in the shade soaking up the peaceful atmosphere and contemplating what he would do about everything.

About a week and a half after he had arrived in Mexico, Necterr noticed a mysterious man kept showing up in the same places as him. The man was usually dressed in expensive business suits, and something about his demeanor made Necterr believe he was from the States even though he appeared to be Mexican. The third time the guy showed up at a beachside bar where Necterr was sipping Coronas, he started to get suspicious. The guy actually nodded to him from across the bar, and Necterr pretended he didn't see it. He downed his beer, paid his tab, and rushed back to his room to pack.

Next he headed north, to Canada. He figured if the mob was trying to track him, they wouldn't look for him there. He had to ditch his clothes from Mexico and buy all new ones once he arrived in Canada. It was too cold there to wear them for one thing, and he didn't want to have to carry more than one bag, so he was trying to continue to pack light. He lived the same way in Canada as he had in Mexico. He first found modest accommodations. This time, his room was decorated in rustic décor, and he laughed to himself as he pulled back the blankets on the bed to find a huge moose staring at him from the pillowcase. He was definitely not in California anymore.

DJ Necterr

Necterr met a few interesting people in Canada, but again, he couldn't be honest with them and usually tried to only hang out with the same people once or twice. He could've pictured becoming good friends with a few of them under different circumstances, but he knew that he was in no position to be making new friends right now. He had already endangered and alienated the friends he had.

Necterr missed his friends and family, but he didn't want to endanger himself or them, so he mostly kept to himself and hoped desperately that everyone he cared about was okay. He wanted to call his parents and let them know that he was okay, but he knew they'd have many questions for them that he couldn't answer, so he would have to wait to talk to them.

When his brother called him, he decided it would be okay to keep in contact with him. Even though he was clear about the fact that he didn't agree with many of the things Necterr had been involved in, he could be trusted, Necterr knew that. He avoided speaking to his sisters much. The last thing he needed was more drama or someone telling him how stupid he'd been. Plus, even though he adored them, he wasn't certain they'd be able to keep his whereabouts a secret. They would want to tell some of his close friends and their parents, and he couldn't have that happening yet.

DJ Necterr

All of Necterr's friends back in the States didn't know where he was, and he kept it that way because he was very worried. He didn't want the mob to be able to track him down, and he didn't want any of his friends to get hurt because they might know where he was. He sadly thought about what had happened to Jerome. He didn't want to be responsible for or connected with any more deaths in his lifetime.

His business was at more than a standstill, and he was starting to get low on funds. He knew he had to make a move before things got really bad and he lost everything he had worked so hard for. After a few months passed, Necterr decided he was tired of hiding. He re-entered the United States, ready to fight to rebuild his business or die trying if necessary.

He didn't have enough of a plan to return home right away; he figured it was best to take things slowly. He went down south to live with his cousin in Tennessee. Necterr felt certain he could trust his cousin and hoped he might even have some suggestions or ideas for how to help. He explained everything to him in detail.

He spent a few months in Tennessee living well and reconnecting with his cousin and with some of his friends and acquaintances from the past. It turned out that a few of these old friends had connections to a big mob from Japan, Korea, or China. He wasn't sure exactly where they were from, and even if he had been sure, he would never tell anyone. It was a secret he would keep to himself forever. This group was very close to the size of the mob that was after him, and they helped him squash his beef with the Italians. Once Necterr was convinced that he was safe, he made plans to finally head home.

By his birthday on December 28, Necterr was finally back home. He threw a huge coming home party combining a New Year's and birthday celebration into one. He was relieved and amazed at the turnout. He had been a little worried that people would still be afraid to be around him, but he realized that events like what had happened to him showed a person who his true friends were. Everyone was happy that he was back and safe. There were some questions asked, but mostly they just all partied and had a great time together just like they had in the past.

Necterr was able to reconnect with his girl. He hadn't realized how much he actually missed her until he saw her at his party. She looked better than ever, and he watched her every move all night long. She was aware of his watching her but seemed to be trying to avoid him. After several drinks, he broke away from some of his closest friends and cornered her. He had to talk to her and find out why she was being so distant. She was ice cold at first, which put Necterr on the defensive. He acted cold toward her, and then decided life was too short, and he would tell her how much he'd missed her and how good it was to be back. She melted. She apologized for her behavior and explained that she had been heartbroken and sick with worry when he disappeared. She couldn't believe he would just take off without explaining why to her.

Necterr explained that it had been for her own good, and that not even his closest friends who had known him forever knew where he was. Their talk ended on a positive note, and she ended up staying with him all night. They had an amazing night together making up for a few months of lost time. It was good to be with her. He couldn't believe how good it felt to be back in a familiar place with someone he knew pretty well. He had no intention of getting serious with any one woman again, but he'd definitely continue to spend time with her. She made him feel secure and needed. These were feelings he really liked after having lived in isolation for several months.

After recovering from his party, Necterr began putting everything into place so he could get himself back into business. He knew he had no time to waste. His connections and business relationships had really suffered, and he would have to work hard to rebuild them once again. He was more than relieved that things could return to normal, but he knew he had a lot of work ahead of him. Once again, he was faced with having to start over. It was okay, though; he knew he could do it, and he loved the challenge! If he had survived a run-in with the mob, he was pretty sure he could do anything he wanted and needed to do. He would put the bad parts of his past behind him again, and use the good parts to recreate his business and life.

All of his fears and insecurities had faded away just like the images of the poor Mexican people and the wide-eyed little boy. He was back home and more than ready to get back to work and start living the good life again. Necterr was confident that business would be thriving again in no time, and that confidence brought a smile to his face.

Chapter 17
Back in Cali

Necterr's beef with the mob was over, but he still had problems with Black Jack. Black Jack didn't like him personally because he knew that Necterr had screwed him over. He now had a personal vendetta against Necterr. He wanted him gone. He made many personal threats toward him. The gist of the threats was that if he ever saw him, he would whoop his ass himself.

Necterr knew deep down that there is never a fair fight, especially with these types of people. Someone always brings their boys; it's never just a one-on-one fight. If he thought it would be one on one with no weapons, he wouldn't have been worried at all. He knew that a fight could escalate to murder in a matter of minutes, though, especially when it was between two bosses. Also, two bosses fighting was never good for business. Every crew member then wants to prove himself too when this happens. The result often ends up being a lot of unnecessary violence.

Every year of his adult life, Necterr had rented out a club and thrown his own birthday party. Since his coming home party had been a success, he decided that this particular year would be no

DJ Necterr

different. He planned to have a bigger bash than ever, inviting everyone he knew and telling them to bring everyone they knew.

When all the plans were in place, he was advised by friends that word on the streets was that he was to die at this birthday party of his. Necterr started hearing from his friends that he should cancel the party, or let it go on but not show up himself. They believed the threats were real, and that he was in great danger. Necterr knew he was in danger, but he had always believed that he should live life to the fullest, and this time was no different. He didn't care about the threats; he was going to have his party.

He found out that Black Jack was good friends with a guy in Cali that a lot of people were afraid of. Necterr knew of him because he had been on and off in the night club scene over the years. They called this man Big, and he was a local street gangster turned promoter. This man stood close to seven feet tall. He was very muscular and was known to be the crazy bipolar type. He was the type to get mad for no reason.

Big caught wind that Necterr had problems with his good friend from Nevada and made himself a part of the beef as well. Big and Black Jack created a plan. The plan was to have Big and his crew attend Necterr's birthday party, kidnap him, and kill him later. There were other rumors about what was supposed to happen to him as well. Some people said that he would get shot while walking into the club; others had heard that he would get shot while leaving the club. He had also heard that there would be a group of guys waiting inside to jump him. Another rumor was that someone would sneak a knife into the club and stab him while he was surrounded by people in the crowd. The rumor about the kidnapping was the one that disturbed him the most because he knew the reputation Black Jack and his associates had for torturing people before killing them.

Necterr's friends, family, and even a woman of his told him this was a party he should either cancel or not attend. Being the man that he was, he did not want to look scared or be called scary, and so he attended this party. He didn't know if it would be his last night alive, or if there would be a shootout, or what would happen. He attended his party with no guards, no vest, no gun, and not a single weapon. He felt at this time that he was ready to go if need be.

He wasn't too worried about his friends, and he didn't have any family there. His friends always knew what they could run into with their type of lifestyles. The friends that didn't have that type of lifestyle were pretty sure that if something was to happen, these guys weren't ruthless gangsters. They knew they would just take out Necterr and try to leave out the innocent bystanders.

DJ Necterr

The day of the party came, and Necterr prayed about whether or not he should show up at his own party or not. He truly felt that his faith on that night would guide him in the right direction. He had seen bullets flying since he was a young child, experienced the loss of friends throughout his life, and had his heart broken by a woman. He felt that if what he was meant to be was dead and headed to a grave, then so be it, it was his time. He only hoped that he would see those he had lost and still missed so much on the other side.

Nothing ever happened at the party. It was a huge success. Many people showed up, including lots of nice-looking women. Necterr pounded drink after drink and reconnected with many friends, some old and some pretty new. Although he had planned the party, he wasn't aware of the huge cake that rolled out onto the stage to the sounds of his friends half-singing, half-screaming happy birthday. It was as tall as he was, and to his surprise, when he went to swipe his hand through the fluffy chocolate cream frosting on the side, two strippers popped up through the top and started singing their own version of the birthday song. After that, Necterr got super drunk and started to party hard with everyone. He had a great night, and though he wouldn't remember all of it, he knew he'd remember the important stuff. He was alive, and no one could touch him. He loved it! He was back in California. He was home.

It turned out that all of the rumors Necterr had heard about his fate if he had attended the party had been just that, rumors. Nobody tried anything, and Necterr never even sensed any sort of danger. He was so glad he had followed his gut and didn't back down. He would never be the kind of person to let others control his actions, and he felt he had proven that once again.

Necterr still received frequent threats from Black Jack, but they really didn't mean anything to him anymore. He would live his life free from fear. Although he hoped to avoid any unnecessary violence, if push ever came to shove, he would stand up and do what he needed to do to protect his family, friends, business, and name.

After the dust settled from the threats and his party, things started really looking up for Necterr again. His brother got married, and he flew out to South Carolina for the wedding. It was on a lovely beach there, and he finally got to see all of his family, including his parents. He had a great weekend reconnecting with all of his family during the days and partying with his cousins at night. He was the one who introduced a few of them to the strip club scene, and they really appreciated that.

Necterr's parents were relieved that he seemed to be doing well and very happy to see him. His mother immediately had tears in her eyes as she hugged him. He'd seen her cry so many times because of him, but this time was different; he could tell they were tears of joy and happiness. She was elated to be with him and able to hug him. It was as if seeing him in person confirmed for her that he was really okay. Though his father wasn't teary, he was also genuinely happy to see him. They talked for a long time about the great experiences he and his mother had in Italy. Necterr then bragged about his business, though he was careful to leave major portions of the truth out, telling his dad only the parts he knew he would want to hear. If his dad had any lingering suspicions about what Necterr was really doing, he was hiding them well.

His family hadn't been together like this for a very long time, and Necterr spent a lot of time getting reacquainted with his parents and his siblings, who were now adults and parents themselves. They asked him a lot of questions about his life, but most of the tension that used to be behind those questions was gone now. It was as though they had either accepted his lifestyle for what they thought it was, or they believed he was doing much better. They could surely tell that he was happier and more at ease than usual, and he knew that this was a relief to his family.

He also enjoyed getting to know the kids and being the cool uncle in their eyes. He tossed a football around with the little ones on the beach, and made a big show of tackling them hard, even though he was as careful and gentle as he could be with them. He caught his brother smiling proudly in his direction as they played together, and Necterr loved the way that felt. He was no longer the dangerous outsider; his family was truly glad to have him there. He was one of them once again. In fact, his brother actually convinced him to stay a week longer so they could spend more time together. Necterr gladly accepted the invitation; not too long before that he would never have imagined his brother wanting to spend any time around him, let alone two weeks.

When he got back home, he felt relaxed and ready to get back to his work and life. He missed his family more than usual after spending that time with them, and he started to wonder what it might be like to have a family of his own someday. Even though he was almost always surrounded by other people, he had that old familiar feeling of loneliness that he had felt a few times in the past, like something was missing in his life.

He was also starting to feel pulled in a different direction, although he didn't understand what direction at the time. He had found the time and resources to follow his favorite football team religiously that season. Watching them play was like an escape from all of the drama of his life. The New England Patriots were going undefeated and heading for the Super Bowl. They were favored to win, and many commentators believed they were near perfection as a team.

DJ Necterr

Watching them play one day a few weeks before the Super Bowl, Necterr started to think about perfection. He knew at that moment that he was destined to reach perfection in his life. He felt that he had reached that point with his business, but something was still out of place or just not right. Deep down inside of him, something started to change. It was a sort of pulling force that he couldn't fully understand. It was always there, from that moment on, and though he tried to ignore it, he couldn't. He wasn't ready to make any major changes to his lifestyle, but he sensed that something needed to change in order for him to truly reach the level of perfection he was meant to reach.

It was then that Necterr started to do a lot of recording. It was for his personal use, so he didn't really put it out to the masses, but he would share it with his close friends when they were riding in the car with him. Everyone who heard his work encouraged him to focus on his music career again. They couldn't believe he wasn't ready to share his recorded work with the world. They all loved it. Their support was encouraging, but Necterr still felt lonely and adrift. His life was going so well that he was baffled by these feelings. He couldn't figure out what was wrong.

Ironically, after a few weeks had passed, Necterr got a few phone calls from Cookie. It was great to hear from her, and they had some great conversations. She updated him on her life, and he told her everything that had been going on with him. Necterr started wondering about reconnecting with her. He wondered if the strange feelings he'd been having had anything to do with her. She expressed her loneliness and the fact that she missed him, but he could tell that she was still holding back and trying not to show a lot of interest. These calls started to make Necterr feel that it was time for a steady woman in his life. Things with Cookie were complicated, though.

The lonely calls from her were hard for Necterr to deal with. Necterr knew that she had screwed him over in the past, but he had forgiven her. He had never been able to win her heart back from her child's father, though. Deep down inside, Cookie knew Necterr was a much better man, but she was fighting the idea of the father not being in her child's life. She was afraid that if she didn't stay with him, he would desert the child also, and she seemed very willing to sacrifice her own happiness for her child.

Though Necterr admired her for caring so much about her child, he thought it was a major waste of her time and life to stay with someone she really didn't want to be with. He also felt that he could be a positive influence in the life of her child if she would let him. He thought back to the hours he had spent playing on the beach with his nephews and what a great time they had together. He wouldn't have minded taking care of Cookie and her child, but he wasn't going to beg her to let him. He relied on his old motto: If it was meant to be, it would be.

Even though they just talked on the phone, Necterr wanted to either see her and move forward or stop talking so frequently because it was hard to go on like that. Finally, Necterr decided that he didn't see her coming back to him. He could tell she was holding back, so he decided he needed to try to move on before he got any more involved with her. He cared about her but really wasn't interested in having a lot of drama in his life, and with the other man still in her life and the hesitation she was apparently feeling, he thought it would be best to walk away. It was hard to do, but he truly believed it was the best for all of them.

Distancing himself from Cookie was hard, and dealing with some of the other feelings he was having made it even harder. There was something wrong, something missing, and he couldn't figure out what it was.

Necterr went to the best place he knew to get a woman off his mind, and that was a strip club. He would not ever admit it, but subconsciously he was looking for a woman that he had had a great connection with in the past. It took a few weeks of spending hundreds and maybe thousands at strip clubs before he finally ran into the beautiful Vivica.

Just as he knew it would be, it was like they had never been apart.

As she had before, Vivica paid for everything and treated Necterr like a king. They spent that night and every night for the next several weeks together. He was very happy with her and proud to be with her. Every time they went somewhere together all eyes were on them. She had a way of drawing a lot attention to herself without even trying whenever she walked into a room.

Necterr loved that he could just be himself around her. He didn't have to worry about her being a gold-digger or being with him for any other dishonest reasons. They always had a great time together, and he felt as if he had known her all his life. She was smart, funny, and extremely sexy. He loved all of those things about her, and the fact that she seemed so completely into him.

Necterr found himself falling hard for Vivica and ignoring all of the other strange feelings he'd been having. He was starting to think maybe she was the one, and settling down with her would make him feel that his life was complete. He didn't realize at that time that he hadn't quite reached perfection in his own life yet, so he wasn't completely ready to share it with another person.

The interesting thing about the relationship that Necterr had with Vivica was that they were both extremely independent. Although this was a quality that had drawn him to her, he sometimes struggled a little with the concept. Necterr was used to getting exactly what he wanted when he wanted it, and he had been with many women who never questioned anything he did or said. Vivica was different. She told it like it was, and wasn't about to be told what to do by anyone. Necterr loved her feisty personality, but he grew more and more uneasy about her lifestyle when they weren't together. He began to feel very possessive of her, and the fact that he couldn't control what happened when they weren't together really bothered him.

For the most part, he kept these feelings to himself. He didn't want to push her away or ruin the fun they were having. He tried to keep a close eye on her, though. It wasn't Vivica he didn't trust; it was the men who frequented the club where she worked. He couldn't trust them—he'd been one of them many times and knew exactly what they were looking for.

Vivica gave him space when he got into his strange moods, which was probably the wisest thing she could have done. She also encouraged him to pursue his first love, his music. She seemed to truly know him so much better than anybody else sometimes. It was as if she could read his mind.

Necterr decided to continue to build his relationship with Vivica and to continue building his business back up to what it had been, while also working to re-establish himself in the music scene. He wasn't sure if he was heading in the right direction, but he had to go with what he knew and with what his gut was telling him. He'd dodged a few bullets and created thousands of memories. He was on good terms with his family again and had a great woman. He hadn't done too bad following his gut instincts so far!

Chapter 18
On Tour with Jay-Z

It was now February 2008, and once again Necterr's business was booming. His friendship with Ashley Mitchell had the potential to expand his business even more, because she wanted to introduce him to artists across the industry. Necterr was open to working with any connections Ashley might have that would allow him to build on what was already a thriving business. Since Ashley was also an assistant to Memphis Bleek, Necterr figured that at some point she would introduce him to Bleek and maybe his best friend, Jay-Z. Before that could happen, Necterr himself was approached by a few of Jay-Z's people. Word had gotten out to a number of artists in the music business about his company, and they wanted to put him into their entourage. They needed a host for after-parties, and because of his reputation, they wanted Necterr to set up these parties. He ended up hosting several after-parties for Jay-Z's artists.

This is when Memphis Bleek became one of his clients. Necterr agreed to set up several parties for Bleek and to make sure that Bleek had protection so that he could attend the parties and feel safe. Being connected to Jay-Z's company was a great feeling at the time. Necterr felt as if he was in the midst of great artists—many of whom produced work he admired. And while being around these artists was an honor, Necterr knew that in the end, it was all about business. His association with Jay-Z's company was just another notch in his surging business and reputation.

All went down successfully at Necterr's parties, and the parties were always nice. Necterr was particular about his work and always wanted things to be just right. For some of his parties, the clubs would be packed with as many as 1,500 people. Everybody would have a good time. There would be no fights and his crew could sell everything they needed to sell. With that many people, the crew could sell 100 to 200 pills a night at ten to fifteen dollars a pill. Necterr easily pulled in three thousand dollars on a night like that. After the party, he would supply the women and friends with the best Ecstasy pills that money could buy. It was nothing but good times.

Necterr's business required him to be on the road a lot, which was tough on his relationship with Vivica. They argued a lot—sometimes over small things. When Necterr returned home from a road trip it wouldn't be long before they would get into another argument. He knew that his being away was part of the reason they were having problems. He tried to make things better by coming home on

Mondays, but by Wednesday, he had to be on the road again. A lot of their arguments were about trust issues. Vivica would get angry because she believed Necterr didn't trust her to do what she needed to do to keep their relationship strong. For one thing she was still stripping, even though she knew Necterr wanted her to stop.

Necterr was adamant about stripping being unhealthy for their relationship. The image of her even pretending to be sexually provocative with other men and acting as if she enjoyed it made him feel queasy in the stomach. Necterr knew that men were turned on by strippers, and he always felt that some men might try to go beyond the tease of the performance and actually approach Vivica. He could hardly stand the thought of some man making a move on Vivica after a performance. It made him mad to think about men who might try to take the situation beyond the point of public entertainment. He could see himself punching out any guy who even looked like he wanted hit on Vivica.

Sometimes Vivica would agree with him. She understood that having an audience of almost all men looking at her bare her body must be tough for Necterr to take. On the other hand, she was confident that most men were afraid to approach her when she wasn't on the stage. Even if they did, Necterr would just have to trust that she would take care of the situation. Tension between them over her stripping was always there because she really wanted to be stripping. Necterr was angry and frustrated about the fact that he couldn't do anything to stop her. Part of him knew that it was hard to live in someone else's shadow when you were also a star. Necterr was getting a lot of respect for his work. She wanted to be in the limelight too. She also wanted to make her own money, like she was able to as a stripper.

Sometimes Vivica turned the tables and got on Necterr about the fact that there were a lot of women around him while he was working his business. Once Necterr came to Vivica's house with a pocket full of money, maybe nine or ten thousand dollars in cash. The money led to a mega argument. They argued because she said when he took off his pants to go to bed he put his money in his socks, and put the socks in bed with him. She wanted to know why he felt he needed to sleep with his money. Before he could say anything she yelled at him that she didn't need to steal his money—that she knew how to make her own money. For her, his thinking that he needed to protect his money was just another indication that Necterr did not trust her. Vivica let him know he was treating her the way you would treat a groupie, or someone you were going to be with for just one night, not someone you called your woman.

In the middle of this argument she told Necterr she knew he was with other women while he was on the road. She believed that there was no way he was around all those women and not sleeping with them. She had her issues about trust with Necterr too. This argument was so intense that Necterr ended up leaving mad—and when he left, Vivica was still mad too. This was not the way he wanted this relationship to be going because for the first time in a while, he really wanted to have one woman to come home to. Necterr went back to the tour, thinking that maybe a little time and distance was a probably a good thing.

About halfway through the tour, a few days before a show scheduled for Atlanta, things took a bad turn. Necterr had decided to make a quick trip back to California before the show. While he often flew back to see Vivica, he also made trips back to Cali to collect money, to make sure the business was running smoothly, or to fix any problems that might have come up while he was doing business out of town. He wouldn't be seeing Vivica on this trip because of the falling out they had after their last argument. As it happened, he had to go through this bad spell without her, although they did get back together a few months after the bad turn of events.

Necterr had arranged for a man who worked for him to pick him up at the airport. The man was there on time, driving a $100k Bentley coupe. Necterr slid into the front seat, feeling good about the fact that his business allowed people who worked for him to show evidence of living the good life. He wasn't aware that the good life for this man not only meant driving a fantastic ride, but also being friendly to women and getting them high. As it turns out, he had been at a house full of women, doing drugs for most of that day. The man had taken several pills just before he arrived at the airport because he also wanted to celebrate with Necterr. That was okay with Necterr—even though he didn't really see this guy as a close friend. At this point in his life there were a lot of people who saw Necterr as their good friend, even though Necterr didn't always see himself as particularly close to those people.

They pulled out of the airport and headed toward the city. The man was talking and socializing like he was really happy about being with Necterr, and he was paying more attention to Necterr than to his driving. Necterr was being sociable and engaging in the conversation with the man, but he was also watching the road. A few minutes into the trip Necterr realized that this guy was very high and was driving way too fast. Suddenly the car started swerving, and as the man tried to regain control, the car skidded off the road, flipped on its side, and came to a halt as they crashed into a building at a gas station.

Amazingly, Necterr remained calm during the accident, which likely prevented him from receiving more injuries than he actually had by the end of the crash. He could see that they were going to hit the building, but it was as if he were just going with the flow of the car's motion. He was slightly high himself and believed this kept his body relaxed as the accident was happening, but then there was the impact. Necterr felt his head hitting just about everything in the car, and then there was stillness. Both Necterr and the driver were able to get out of the car without being in too bad a shape. Necterr had injuries to his head, but beyond that his injuries were minor and there were no broken bones.

He heard sirens in the distance, and it wasn't long before the police arrived. As they were looking over the accident, the police noticed that there was alcohol in the back seat that had smashed all over the car from the impact of the crash. The presence of alcohol at the scene of an accident meant they had to conduct a more thorough investigation. The police probably thought alcohol had something to do with the accident, since the driver's eyes were glossy and he was leaning on a police car in a daze, looking as if he had no idea where he was or how he got there.

Necterr wasn't worried about the search the police were conducting because it is not a crime to have alcohol in your car. Neither Necterr nor the driver had been drinking alcohol; there just happened to be some in the back of the car. As the police conducted their search, it wasn't long before Necterr realized that he had been riding with the stupidest man ever. This guy had about twenty-four pills in the car for his personal use, not having enough sense to leave the pills at the house where he had spent most of the day getting high. Of course the police found the pills. The man was immediately arrested, and because of his record, Necterr was arrested too.

Even though the driver was charged, Necterr was not initially charged with anything. Getting arrested was not a big deal for him. He was used to these trips to jail by now, and besides, he knew he would be out within a matter of hours. Necterr also wasn't too worried that this incident would result in any complications for his business. Because investigators and FBI agents kept his business under a microscope, he had made sure there were protections in place—such as making sure nothing was in his name. The car in the accident and his tour bus, however, were both in the name of the same female. It didn't take the investigators long before they were able to connect the dots. They informed Necterr that they needed to seize additional items of his property as evidence in order to complete the investigation. They were even planning to take Necterr's tour bus.

At first, Necterr was devastated. The tour bus was a big part of the way he conducted business. Even though he traveled by plane with the artists, he had a crew traveling to the tour site on the bus, and the bus had a stash full of pills for people at his parties. Having the bus itself seized would not ruin his business, but it was an inconvenience. Not having the bus meant he would just have to find another way to stash pills. At the same time, he knew that if drugs were found on the bus while it was in the possession of the police, his business would be destroyed and he would go to jail for a long time. He was thinking that the investigators might just take the bus and dust it for prints or something like that. If that was the case, he figured he would get the bus back in a few days. But Necterr was in the habit of thinking about all possibilities, and he was thinking that the investigators would most likely look for anything and everything they could find on the bus that would give them enough evidence to put him away. Luckily, having prior notice that the bus would be seized gave Necterr enough time to have his crew clear out the bus so that the investigators would find nothing to implicate him. He still had the problem of having no tour bus to travel with and to carry his stuff. This is when he and Bleek had a falling out.

Bleek had two security guards who protected him at the after-parties. In addition to setting up the party, it was Necterr's job to get the two security guards to the place where the party was happening so that they could protect Bleek. Necterr normally had the security guards travel on his bus. Since the bus was being seized, he had to find another way to transport them. He decided to fly the security guards to the shows and after-parties. This would be an additional expense, but that was okay because he wanted the bus seizure to disrupt his business as little as possible. Ashley informed Necterr that if he had to fly the security guards, he would have to let the airlines know that the security guards would be traveling with guns, since they were South Carolina cops.

South Carolina cops! It wasn't until then that Necterr realized that the two security guards were actually cops. All this time, he had been transporting cops on his bus! Dealing with cops was not good for his business, and Necterr was not excited about working with or around them. Besides, he had never trusted cops. Given the nature of his business, he thought Bleek could have at least let him know that the guards were cops. Still, he had a business arrangement with Bleek and was willing to hold up his end of the understanding. Part of being successful in this business was being trusted to do what you said you would do.

The tour was a few days away from California when Necterr talked to Bleek about being part of a big event with Jay-Z that would take place in California. Necterr knew safety was a big issue for Bleek, and that he would not want to go anywhere without protection. But Necterr really didn't want to fly the cops to California. He preferred to have his own security make sure that Bleek was safe. He promised Bleek that he would provide him with high quality security and assured him that the protection would be the very best anyone could ask for. Bleek turned down the offer, saying that California was just too dangerous. He used as an excuse that in a place as dangerous as California, he really needed to have his own security guards with him. Necterr tried to convince Bleek that he would be safe in California with security handpicked by him. When Bleek wouldn't budge, Necterr promised him extra money so that if he wanted to fly the cops out to California, he could. Necterr wanted nothing to do with the guards now that he knew they were cops. If Bleek wanted to fly them in, Necterr was willing to finance the trip as a way of upholding his agreement with Bleek of ensuring protection. Bleek was not interested in hearing about any of the arrangements Necterr was attempting to make for protection or, for that matter, any of the events Necterr was planning. He canceled all of his after-parties and kicked Necterr off the tour.

Necterr was stunned. Just like that, Bleek had severed all their connections and arrangements. He couldn't understand why Bleek first refused to work with him on the security issue and then totally removed him from the tour. His bewilderment soon turned to anger and suspicion. Bleek's behavior and this whole thing about working around cops had Necterr spooked. Now he wondered if his bus was seized because of the accident or if the cops he had been transporting on his bus were actually working undercover. He wondered if it was just a coincidence that his bus was seized or if this was all a setup to try to bring him down. And now, Bleek no longer wanted to party with him.

Necterr ended up putting the party together anyway and it was a huge success. A few of his famous friends showed up and everyone had a good time. Being around friends witnessing his skill at hosting another successful party made Necterr feel good for the moment— in spite of this situation with Bleek. Pills were sold at the party, money was made, and everyone seemed pretty happy. But Necterr's Jay-Z and Rocafella "thing" with Bleek was over. There were no more parties scheduled and Necterr was no longer a part of Jay-Z's artists' company.

Necterr shared his suspicions about Bleek and the cops with a few people, still having difficulty believing that the turn of events was purely coincidental. It was hard for him to get around the fact that he had trusted and worked with someone who could cut him off so easily and quickly—especially at a time when there was so much suspicion about this person's familiar ways with cops. The whole deal was even further tainted by the fact that Bleek had been paid for the shows that he later missed, and he didn't refund the money. This whole situation smelled pretty rank to Necterr. Bleek was a big name in the world of hip-hop, but that didn't give him the right to dishonor promises and treat people with disrespect. Necterr thought people should know just what kind of person Bleek was. He would normally have sent his crew out to deliver the message, but when someone was in the spotlight like Bleek was, it was hard to send a message that would reach the people who needed to hear it.

Necterr thought that people like Bleek must feel like they are untouchable—that they can do anything they wanted to do, and there would be no pushback. Bleek not returning the money made Necterr angry at first. But the written word that speaks the truth is powerful and can carry a message far beyond what can be communicated face to face from one person to the next. Necterr's anger pushed him to return to a practice he had used often in his life when a situation threatened to get him down. He put his emotions on paper and wrote a song to expose Bleek's rank actions.

"You took my money u got my 5 stacks/ you broke dude man you can have that." The words felt freeing to Necterr. Some of the tension and anger he was feeling about the whole situation began to fade away. If the money meant that much to him—if Bleek needed the money that badly, then he should keep it. In retrospect, the amount of money was not a big deal for Necterr. Five grand was chump change. Necterr pulled in that amount and sometimes more in one day. He could also lose five grand in a day at the casino—so he just decided to look at the money Bleek kept as a night at the casino. He didn't know this when he first hooked up with Bleek, but as it turned out, it was a gamble to even associate with him. Necterr took multi-thousand-dollar losses gambling all the time. In the end, it really wasn't about the amount of money Bleek snatched. It was more about the principal of the thing—that this high profile "artist" could renege on a gig and then just keep the money. Necterr pushed the "diss" song forward hard. People needed to know about Bleek. They needed to know about the man in the spotlight who ducks behind the scenes and takes what does not belong to him.

Chapter 19
The Deal of a Lifetime

few months had passed since Necterr's ordeal with Bleek and his cops, and the confiscation of his tour bus. He had been able to remove the scum called Memphis Bleek off his list of things that were important to him at this point in his life. He'd also found ways to deal with his bus being seized. Not having the bus was an inconvenience, but it by no means shut down the business. Transportation for local deals was not an issue. For out-of-state deals, Necterr was able to rent a van to transport his product. As a result, Necterr's business continued to thrive. He had established a strong base of business associates which included a large number of return customers. Even though business was booming, Necterr was always open to opportunities to expand. An unbelievable opportunity presented itself when he was on a trip to Canada.

Necterr was in Canada exploring the clubs, DJing some of the time, but making plenty of time to have some fun. He ran into a woman named Ebony at one of these clubs. Vivica had introduced him to Ebony a while back when they were partying at a club in the States. Ebony and Necterr were having a good time and enjoying each other's company. It was well into their conversation when Ebony let Necterr know that she worked for the biggest drug dealer in Canada. Necterr just smiled at first, not knowing if he should take seriously what he was hearing or not. Ebony continued to talk about her boss and said she would be willing to arrange a meeting, if Necterr was interested. He was listening a little closer now, but his first reaction was that this guy probably had mob ties in order to have the type of business Ebony was describing. Necterr was not interested in dealing with the mob or Mafia again. The pain of losing Jerome to the mob and living under threats to his life from Jerome's mob associates was enough to convince him never to do business with the mob again. He had learned to conduct a highly successful business without working with people who thought nothing of taking your life if they didn't like the way a business deal had gone down.

Ebony assured Necterr that her boss had no ties to any mob or Mafia. This man was his own boss and only answered to himself. According to Ebony, this could be a very profitable business relationship for both Necterr and her boss. Necterr thought that he would be willing to at least meet this man, and if everything he was being told about this guy was true, he would consider doing business with him.

It only took a few days for a meeting to be arranged between Necterr and the Canadian drug dealer. Even the setup of the meeting had Necterr wondering about the type of business deal he was about to get into. The Canadian drug dealer flew Necterr to the meeting at his home in a private jet. Necterr knew that this guy must have serious money if he was able to afford his own jet. He was immediately impressed, although he was not quite sure he could trust what was going on. Here he was, flying in a private jet to meet a man he had not even heard of before. Still, he was just beginning to explore the Canadian market, so not knowing this dealer wasn't that big of a deal. He didn't know what this man had heard about him, but it must have been something pretty extraordinary or the guy would not be going through all of this trouble to meet him. That was the second thing that impressed Necterr. This dealer seemed to be going out of his way to meet him.

Necterr slept through most of the plane ride. He was being escorted by three men who he figured were part of the drug dealer's crew. After the plane landed, Necterr was taken to the most fabulous house he had ever seen; in fact, this was more than just a house—this was a mansion. As he entered the hallway of the mansion, a beautiful black woman dressed in a white halter and scandalously tight red shorts approached him. Necterr noticed big hazel eyes set against a beautiful dark caramel complexion. She placed her firm body next to his in a welcoming embrace, and as she stepped back, Necterr could see that her broad smile revealed a set of deep dimples. She took Necterr's hand and led him across marble floors and through glass double doors to a pool area, which was full of more beautiful women. Necterr was thinking he had just arrived at an international convention of sexy and beautiful women. While there were a lot of black women around the pool, there were also women from every background imaginable. They were all dressed like the woman who had greeted him, and the men who were lounging around the pool with these women appeared to be enjoying their company. He later learned that the "Boss," which was what everybody called him, kept a cadre of strippers and porn stars around him for private performances and other types of entertainment.

Everyone around the pool seemed to be relaxed in this luxury. As Necterr took a moment to take in his surroundings beyond the sea of beautiful women, he noticed Ebony walking toward him. She flashed him a warm smile and when she reached him, she gently grabbed his arm and told him he could return to the pool side and Ericka (with the big hazel eyes) later. First, there was business to take care of, and the Boss was waiting. She led him through another set of double doors, to an elevator that took them to a second floor. The first thing Necterr noticed when he entered the upstairs room was the wall of windows that faced a huge yard of neatly cut lawn that sloped down to what must have been a private beach area. The second and last thing that grabbed all of Necterr's attention during the total length of the meeting was the man Ebony referred to as the "Boss," and more of his crew.

The men in this room did not have the relaxed look of the men around the pool. Their bodies were tense as they moved around the room in slow, deliberate motions, almost as if they did not want to draw too much attention to themselves. When the Boss rose from his chair to greet Necterr, two or three men who had been sitting jumped to their feet as well, as if some kind of royalty had just risen from his throne. The crew switched their glances back and forth from the Boss to Necterr the whole time Necterr was in the room. And it wasn't as if they looked at the Boss directly; glances in his direction were more like looks out of the side of their eyes. You could tell that the men in this room either feared or respected—maybe both—this man called Boss. You could definitely see the fear in their eyes. Necterr figured the glances toward him were meant to size him up—to figure out what this young dude was all about.

The Boss himself was one scary dude. Right away it was clear to Necterr that even though this man was not associated with the mob, he was the kind of person you would not want to cross. As he approached Necterr, the Boss smiled, but the smile only reached the right side of his mouth so that it looked more like a smirk than a smile. The Boss had deep-set eyes and a constant gaze. Necterr thought to himself, this guy doesn't even blink! He just glared with that half smile. As he talked, he paused after every few sentences and gave you that glare—as if he wanted to see that you were taking in everything he was saying. The Boss grabbed Necterr's hand for a handshake. Necterr felt as if his hand had been snared by a human vise-grip. The Boss' handshake was more than just firm. This handshake wasn't too far away from an arm wrestle—the kind meant to bring you to your knees. But Necterr wasn't going to fold in front of this guy. He gripped the dealer's hand firmly in return. In a weird kind of way, the dealer seemed to appreciate this unspoken message of matched strength.

The Boss invited Necterr to have a seat in a plush high-back chair that faced the one where the Boss had been sitting. He told Necterr about his business in Canada, much of which was a repeat of what Ebony had told him. The Boss sold Ecstasy throughout the whole country—if you did X pills in Canada, you got them from him. He went on to tell Necterr that his business was very organized and his crew knew how to get product to different parts of the country without any difficulty at all. His problem was that he did not have the volume of product needed to address the demand. That was why he was interested in talking with Necterr. He had been looking for a reliable supplier for a long time. The Boss talked a little about his ties to casinos and other businesses in Vegas, but his main reason for wanting to meet Necterr was to see if he could supply him with pills for his Canada operation.

Necterr and the Boss talked for about an hour to make sure that the business arrangement they were creating would be profitable for both of them. After their conversation, the Boss told Necterr he could stay at the house while he was arranging for the flow of pills to begin. Wearing his half smile, he told Necterr that he could make use of all that his "humble home" had to offer—women, food, drink—anything that Necterr needed. He also offered his crew, letting both Necterr and the crew know in one set of directives that he expected all would run smoothly. They shook hands firmly again, and as Necterr headed toward the elevator, it dawned on him that he still did not know this man's name—other than "Boss." In fact, to this day, he still does not know the Boss' name.

On the ride down the elevator, another realization hit Necterr. He had probably just made the biggest deal of his life. The thought left him ecstatic. He tried to calculate in his head the amount of money he would bring in, but the figure was just too big. He would have to wait until morning to get a better feel for the amount of money tied to this deal. Necterr made his way back to the pool to enjoy the evening and the company of Ericka. He was trying to take in the events of the day; in some ways the day was unbelievable. But here he was in these luxurious surroundings, a sexy and beautiful woman by his side, and a fantastic deal in his back pocket.

The next morning Necterr began the work of setting his crew in motion so that pills could be delivered to Canada as quickly as possible. He contacted his supplier in the States and warned him that this was going to be a huge order. Since he no longer had the bus, he had to be creative in terms of getting the pills to Canada. He figured he might still be hot if his suspicions were right about Memphis Bleek's cops being undercover. He needed to make sure that not too much attention was drawn to him or his crew. Necterr was able to make all the necessary arrangements to sell the Boss 500,000 pills in their first deal. He ended up working with the Boss for a number of weeks, making the same deal with him over and over again.

The money was coming in fast—almost too fast. In a matter of weeks, Necterr had become a multimillionaire. He knew he needed to be smart about how to handle this amount of money. Banks were not an option. He would only leave small amounts of money in banks for a short period of time, most times no more than twenty-four hours. Necterr hated dealing with small street banks because he didn't trust that they could keep his money safe. All anyone needed to do in order to break into a safe at a small bank was to get a code. He also wanted to avoid problems with the Internal Revenue Service. Necterr did not want to provide the IRS with a paper trail that would lead back to him. Depositing and withdrawing huge sums of money was a perfect sign to the IRS that money was tied to some type of drug deal.

The solution for Necterr was to keep his money with him, so he carried his money around in a duffel bag. Sometimes he had as much as $750,000 to $900,000 in his bag. The rapid and continuous flow of money from the Canadian sales made him feel heady with success. After a short period of time, Necterr was very comfortable carrying money around in his bag. He felt untouchable, and carrying a bag full of money around did not bother him at all.

Necterr was making a lot of money, but he also was spending a lot of money. He was living a life of luxury—buying clothes, paying cash for a condominium, entertaining women, and hiring drivers for the expensive luxury cars he rented. If he wanted to stay in a hotel, he chose the grandest and most expensive hotel available. Most of the time he didn't even bother to check how expensive something would be; he knew he had enough money to take care of it. Necterr spent some of his money on his friends. If they were late for car notes,

Necterr took care of the bill for them. If he was out with friends, he usually footed the whole bill. Being with friends and enjoying himself at clubs was one of Necterr's favorite things to do. The deal of a lifetime had made him a rich man—and he was living like one.

It was during this time that he and Vivica got back together. They had been on again and then off for what seemed like a very long time. Necterr still liked being with her and she liked being with him too. If there was such a thing as a soul mate, Vivica was his. As soon as they got back together, they fell into their familiar and comfortable ways of being with each other. Being with Vivica felt good—especially when they were able to avoid getting into arguments. Sometimes they would hang out at the clubs with other friends and just have a good time. Other times they would hang out at the condo all night, listening to music or watching TV and getting high.

Necterr had gotten into using cocaine to the point that it had become a huge problem. The word on the street was that you couldn't get hooked on coke. Necterr now knew that was a lie—he couldn't seem to stop himself from using the stuff. Getting high on coke was one of the things he and Vivica did together. They would snort coke, have a few drinks, and when they started to lose their buzz, they would snort some more. With all the money he was making, he could buy as much coke as they could possibly want. There was a lot about his life that he couldn't share with his family. The problem he had with coke was one of those things. He hid his cocaine problem from everyone in his family.

Necterr was generally very careful about how he handled drugs for his personal use. He took extra precautions to make sure the police never caught him carrying drugs. He of course wanted to take the same precautions for his girl, but there was one unintended slip-up. Necterr was at a club waiting for Vivica to arrive when his cell phone rang. It was Vivica and she was in jail. She had been stopped by police on her way to the club. They told her they clocked her driving forty miles an hour in a thirty-mile-an-hour zone. After they stopped her, they searched the car and found drugs Necterr had left in the car the night before. She was being charged with possession of Ecstasy and cocaine.

When Necterr reached the jail to post bail, one look at Vivica told him that she was mad—real mad. He couldn't tell if she was mad at him, mad about being arrested, or mad that she had been charged with possession—maybe all of these things contributed to her anger. Even so, she had not turned on him. She could have easily snitched on him and let the police know that the drugs were not hers. Instead, she accepted the charges. Whether the cops would have believed her or not, just her saying that the drugs belonged to Necterr would have been enough for them to arrest him—an arrest they would have relished.

Necterr wanted to let Vivica know he was sorry she had gotten caught with his drugs. He took her on a one hundred thousand dollar spending spree at a California casino. Necterr had the money to spend and did not worry about whether they were winning or losing. He was just having a very good time with someone who had looked out for him. Being a multimillionaire had changed his life in so many ways. A lot of people knew about him and they knew the nature of his business. His name on the streets had become as big as a true drug boss. Necterr had old friends, many work associates, and old and new enemies. He had to be more careful about whom he trusted. He had two bodyguards whom he trusted with his life. He also had Vivica. Her decision to quietly accept the drug arrest took their relationship to a new level. Knowing what could have happened had she snitched on him made him trust her even more. Necterr thought it interesting that so many of their arguments in the past were about trust issues—her mistrusting him when it came to other women and him mistrusting her when it came to other men. But when a situation came about that could have led to more time in prison, Vivica acted in the best interest of Necterr. He now trusted her as one of the people in his world who cared about his well-being.

Chapter 20
They Forced My Hand

Everybody on the street knew Necterr's drug business was lucrative. They also knew he had a habit of walking around with a duffel bag full of money. He was an easy target for robbers because it was also a known fact that only two people provided him security. There were a number of attempted robberies but none were successful. Necterr enjoyed the status of being a successful drug boss who was pretty much untouchable. He felt good about the way things were going in his life right now.

His relationship with Vivica was also going well, and they spent a lot of time together. One evening they decided not to hit the clubs; they wanted to have an evening at the condo with just the two of them. Necterr had taken a shower and was in the upstairs bedroom getting dressed. Vivica was downstairs in the living room watching TV when she thought she heard someone at the door. She called to Necterr upstairs to ask who he was expecting as she walked to the door to see who was there. She opened the door, looked outside, but could see no one. As she was about to close the door three men burst into the condo and pinned

Vivica against the wall. Necterr heard the scuffle and Vivica's scream.

He ran downstairs and as he reached the door, one of the guys grabbed him from behind. Necterr elbowed him in the ribs and swung around to deliver a powerful blow to the guy's midsection. As the man crumpled to the floor, Necterr ran back toward the stairs that led to the second floor of the condo. He knew he had to get to the gun he kept in the bedroom. The man holding Vivica threw her to the floor, and two of the men chased Necterr up the stairs. Necterr heard gunshots as he made the turn on the second floor landing. Seconds later he felt a searing pain in his leg; he knew he had been shot. The bullets kept flying as a second bullet grazed the wrist that covered his forehead. Necterr made it to his bedroom and grabbed his gun. He could hear the men approaching in the hall near the bedroom door. He ran out of the bedroom shooting and then headed to the third floor of the condo. The men first turned toward the stairs to the second floor to avoid Necterr's shots, but quickly turned again toward the third floor in their pursuit of him. Necterr ran into the room where glass doors led to the balcony. He could hear the men coming into the room, so he decided to jump from the balcony. At this point he was sure it was him they wanted—and not Vivica. If he could keep them chasing him, he figured she would be okay. Necterr landed first onto a row of bushes on the ground level of the condo and then rolled over into the street.

He was thinking that this felt more like a hit than a robbery. There was money in the condo, and if these men only wanted money, why did they try to rob him when they knew someone was in the condo? Necterr knew he had to get as far away from the condo as he could. His leg and wrist were bleeding profusely now, and although every move brought excruciating pain, Necterr began to run down the street. He ran to a car that was waiting for the light to change, and banged on the passenger side window. He was bleeding so badly that the window was immediately covered with blood. Necterr moved around the front of the car to the driver's side, trying to get the woman driver to lower her window. He could see the horror in her eyes. The woman sped off, leaving Necterr in the street, exposed to the men he figured would come gunning for him in any minute.

Necterr ducked into more bushes to give himself time to think about what to do next. When he moved his wrist to alleviate some of the pain, his hand brushed his pant pocket and he realized he had his cell phone with him. He called a friend but no one answered. Necterr next called 911 for an ambulance. He did not want to be caught with a gun, so he managed to dig a hole in the dirt behind the bushes and stash it. He lay there bleeding and in pain as he waited for what seemed like a very long time for the ambulance to reach him. The police arrived with the ambulance and he let them know that Vivica might still be in the condo. He was taken to the hospital, but the police went back to the condo. Vivica was still there, pretty shaken by everything that had happened. The police brought her to the hospital to have her bruises looked at and to also let her check on Necterr. Before long she was in the emergency room with him until he was taken to surgery to have the bullet removed from his leg.

A group of police stayed at the condo to investigate what they were now calling a burglary. Even though the incident felt like a hit to Necterr, according to the police, the main motive for the break-in was robbery. The police speculated that the robbers panicked—thinking that the noise of gunshots would bring the police—and left the condo area empty-handed. In the process of searching the condo, the police found a piece of paper which had apparently been dropped by one of the robbers as he was fleeing. Necterr's name and address appeared on the paper, and so did the name and address of his right-hand man, Felipe. The investigators immediately turned their attention to Felipe and sent police to his house to supposedly investigate or ward off a possible burglary. Felipe was home when the police arrived. He became nervous and anxious when the police told him he was possibly a target for a burglary. They questioned Felipe and told him they wanted to come in to make sure everything was okay. Felipe could not stop them from looking around the house.

When he thought about it later, Necterr was sure the police saw an opportunity to get to him through Felipe. They found a way to get a warrant right away and began a more thorough search of Felipe's house. It didn't take them long to find the huge stash of drugs in the house, and they probably believed the stash had to belong to Necterr. Felipe was arrested on the spot, but the police did not come for Necterr that evening. Necterr was still in the hospital when he received a call from Felipe's sister. She sounded both desperate and angry at the same time. She wanted to know what had gone down, and who led the police to her brother. Necterr told her to meet him in the afternoon the next day at a restaurant located on a corner near a club the three of them had frequented. They needed to talk about what had happened and how to get Felipe out of jail.

Necterr was released from the hospital the next morning, since the bullet had not gone through his leg. He was still in pain, but he was determined to meet Felipe's sister so that they could try to make some sense out of what had happened the night before. Necterr and Felipe's sister were just beginning to talk when Necterr noticed two men walking toward them. He knew that look—suits with an overly confident smugness about them.

Necterr and Felipe's sister were arrested by the two FBI agents. For just the briefest of seconds he wondered how the FBI agents knew he would be at this particular restaurant at this particular time. He was pretty sure informants had not given them the information, although he knew there were snitches out there. No—this arrest wasn't caused by the work of an informant—the FBI probably had been following him since he left the hospital that morning.

The Feds had intensified their efforts and were working with the local police and the Drug Enforcement Administration to build a case against Necterr. Sometimes they would find reasons to come to his house to ask a whole series of questions, and would sometimes approach his friends in their homes to ask questions about drugs and drug deals. The calls and questions had really gotten out of hand, but Necterr did not know how to stop the Feds' intrusions. Necterr also had the feeling he was being watched and followed more closely since the car accident. The FBI tried to be incognito, but Necterr had become good at spotting them. Once, a bakery van was parked across the street from his condo daily for at least a week. The Feds were not as smart as they were made out to be. Necterr knew the van housed undercover agents since there were no bakeries within twenty miles of the condo. His belief that he was under close surveillance was confirmed when the agents appeared at the restaurant. Necterr figured the FBI thought they finally had enough evidence to put him in prison for a very long time.

The FBI was thwarted once again. Necterr ran his business so well that they had nothing to hold him on, so they had to release him. Even though Felipe's sister was involved with the business, they had much less on her, and she ended up being released as well. Felipe, however, was still being held, but he was not talking. While they were short on evidence, the FBI was long on threats. They told Necterr they were working on using the RICO law to throw him in prison for life. They were looking to find evidence to charge him with multiple counts of racketeering, which came with a fine of $25,000 and a twenty-year sentence per count. When they finished with him, they were going to go after his family members and prove that they were working with his drug business. These agents knew where and how to hit hard. Necterr had heard about the RICO law, but he also heard that the Feds often threaten people with it to try to get the accused to fold and plead guilty to lesser chargers. He didn't know what was true at this point, but he wasn't going to say anything to these guys. One thought kept creeping into his mind— after all his efforts to stay away from the Mafia, the Feds were throwing the same law at him that they used to lock up Mafia members.

It was late evening by the time Necterr returned home from jail. His leg was aching and his head felt like it was going to split open. He felt as though he was being attacked from all sides. The Feds were pursuing him, but he was also being pursued and betrayed by people he knew. As it turned out, one of the robbers from the previous night's attempt was his friend Ramon's brother. Necterr could not figure out how he was supposed to have seen that one coming. The robbers had enough information about him to feel that they could successfully rob him. But there were snitches and connivers all around him. He thought about the time an agent tried to get him to implicate himself as a dealer by telling him that Lil Wayne and his manager Cortez had already given statements about his criminal activities. Necterr also knew that his associates were giving up information about the location and nature of his deals. He felt distraught over the fact that he thought he could trust people who would give him up to the Feds or any dog on the street who wanted to rob him. And now the Feds were talking about going after his family. As he thought more about what was going on in his life, he began to realize that even though he had made a lot of money, his business had done nothing but put him on the run. He had risked his life for the business, and now the business was putting his family's life at risk too.

Necterr felt an overwhelming sense of sadness as he thought more about how he had been betrayed. He agonized over the thought that his enemies—enemies from the street, cops, the Feds —would try to get to him by hurting his family, but he couldn't think of a way to keep them safe. He felt his family was disappointed in him, so he had kept his distance. But he loved his family and would not want to be the reason for them being harmed. Suddenly Necterr felt as if his whole body was in unbearable pain—his leg and head ached; his chest felt heavy. He felt he was being dragged under by feelings of despair. Necterr was thinking he needed a really good high to lift him out of the overpowering pain that was engulfing him. He needed something to numb these awful feelings.

He made his way to the stash of drugs he kept hidden in the kitchen and then climbed the stairs to the bedroom. He sat on the floor and took two pills, and then two more. The pain was still there. He was determined to find the high that would rid him of the agony he was in—or he would die trying. He lined the pills up in a straight row, pretending they were Skittles. He began to take them one by one, duping himself into believing that the sweetness of the pretend candy pills would replace the bitterness he was feeling. He took three more pills; then three more. The pain was starting to go away. He felt good for a minute, but then the pain in his chest returned. Necterr popped five pills into his mouth at once. On some levels he knew what he was doing—overdosing on his drugs was one way to keep his enemies away from him and his family. He had swallowed at least fifteen pills in about five minutes. Necterr could feel his heart pounding—pressure was building in his chest. He felt as if his head and chest were about to explode. He was cold and shivering uncontrollably, but his shirt was soaked with sweat. Necterr was floating in and out of consciousness as scenes from his life appeared and then faded way. As he keeled over on the floor, the last thing he heard was Vivica screaming his name.

Vivica had been out most of the day but arrived to the darkened condo around eight. She saw light coming from the bedroom and called to Necterr as she walked up the stairs. She gasped as she saw him lying motionless on the floor. She ran to Necterr's side and began to shake him as she screamed his name. Necterr was able to open his eyes for the briefest of moments—just long enough to see the shock on Vivica's face. By now Necterr was struggling to breathe, so Vivica knew he was not dead. She grabbed her cell phone from her bag and called 911. She noticed the row of pills close to Necterr's body. He must have been getting high from a bad batch of drugs. Vivica did not know what to do while she waited for the ambulance, so she sat on the floor and placed Necterr's head in her lap. There she sat, gently stroking the side of his face and slowly rocking back and forth as silent tears streamed down her face.

Necterr was reborn the day he nearly died. Like any birth, the journey to life takes time, and there are struggles along the way. He was semiconscious by the time they reached the hospital. Fortunately, doctors were able to remove the drugs from his body, and he was in recovery for several months after he left the hospital. For a while he needed complete bed rest. Then he progressed to a wheelchair, then to crutches. He needed several surgeries and there was damage to his heart that required medication. These remedies were going to help him recover from the physical chaos caused by taking his drugs.

Necterr also needed to recover from the years of pain and mental anguish that led him to the night when he filled his body with drugs. This would take time also. While in the recovery process, Necterr realized he did not want to die. As importantly, he knew he had the power within him to stay alive. He had a lot of time to think about the type of life he wanted to live.

Vivica stuck with Necterr through most of his recovery. He was well aware of the fact that had she not come home when she did, he would not be making the kinds of decisions he was making about his life. After he was able to get around without the use of a wheelchair, Vivica left.

DJ Necterr

Necterr and Vivica had a complicated relationship. They had been through a lot together and had the kind of attachment to each other that cannot be easily explained. Necterr was unable to figure out why she decided to leave when she did, but her departure was not going to keep him from pursuing a new life. One important part of reshaping your life is to take stock of your social landscape, and sometimes you have to separate yourself from people and activities that were a part of the past lifestyle. While it was clear he had to let go of his drug business, the reality was that he had to let certain people go as well.

The mainstay on his journey of rebirth was his family. Reconciliation with his parents meant a lot to him. He didn't want to run or hide his life from them anymore. They were with him throughout the recovery process. He could see two things in their eyes when he first saw them after the overdose. First there was a message of love—a message that said you are our son—no matter what. The second look spoke to the sadness they felt about Necterr's attempt to take his life. Still, they embraced his desire to take a different path and were supportive of Necterr in whatever ways he needed them to be. When he needed to have surgery, his father was there to make sure he had a way to and from the hospital. His mother was there to take him wherever he needed to go also—and to make sure his day-to-day needs were taken care of.

Necterr turned to the church to support his transition to a new way of life, and his parents willingly made sure he was able to attend church each Sunday. He found going to church gave him time to meditate and think about the life he wanted. He thought a lot about the role drugs had played in his life. The drugs he took did not kill him—he decided that he would not allow selling drugs to kill him either.

It would be dishonest to say that he did not miss some parts of his previous life as a successful drug boss, but Necterr was the perfect gangster. Everyone knows you can't get better than perfect. Being the perfect gangster wasn't only about perfecting the craft while he lived the gangster lifestyle. In 2007, the New England Patriots went undefeated during the season and everyone thought they were invincible. If they had won Super Bowl XLII they would have been a team of perfection, but they lost. Perfection is not only what you do during the season; it is also about what happens in the end. A gangster can run a smooth and successful business—but he can perfect his craft by surviving and choosing to get out of the lifestyle. In the end, that is what Necterr chose to do—he was truly The Perfect Gangster.

There are cues given throughout our lives of what is possible for us—we just have to pay attention to them. When Necterr decided to leave the streets, he was more open to the cues that would provide direction for his next journey to perfection.

He thought about all the parties he had hosted and it dawned on him that one thing he really liked about hosting parties was being around the artists. And so there it was. Perhaps he saw a reflection of himself when he witnessed artists deep into their music and performance. He'd always suspected that hip-hop would be a part of his life, and now he was open to pursue it. There was one more thing he had to do. He had a story scratching around in his head and he wanted to put it down on paper—*"The stress is swallowing him whole..."*

Acknowledgments

I would first like to thank the Lord for saving me in every situation. I do believe that I would not still be here if it were not for Him.

My mother and my father for putting up with a bunch of my BS, lies, and everything else I have done. My brother for always keeping it real with me and holding no punches when it came to telling me like it is. My two sisters—next to my mother y'all are my favorite women in the world. I love you two. My nephews and niece—you guys keep me working hard every day. I have no kids so you guys are my babies. Uncle loves y'all. My brother from another mother, Q. Love you, homie. Thanks for all the help in life. Sara, thank you for putting up with Q and giving him such a beautiful baby. My sister-in-law...you know who you are! Big Country—I love you, too. I want to give a shout out to the team that started it all—LoeDown Enterprises...aka...you know who y'all are. Thanks to my manager B for taking every call and putting the effort to make everything a success. The whole 4 Starz crew—I love y'all. Success is in our future. Hey, E! Good looking for always making sure ya boy is right. Oh, and Miss and Meeka good looking for making sure I am at every event. To my agent for believing in me...Mrs. Tiffany Durant...thank you. My booking agent, Monstah, thank you for putting me at the biggest shows in Cali. I love all you guys and thank you for the support and dealing with my funky ways. We are headed to the top! To all the women I have dealt with—I am sorry. To the two loves of my life—Cookie and Vivica—I still love you both, and I am sorry to you two as well. RIP to the best manager I ever had. You inspired this whole book, so for that, Jerome, you know I'll always love you. Uncle Ted, I am truly your brother's son. RIP and I pray that I can do better one day.

To my fans, friends and everyone else who has supported me, thank you, and I love you all too. I am nothing without y'all!

DJ Necterr

LaVergne, TN USA
20 February 2011
217229LV00001B/114/P